Scripture Discussion Commentary 5

SCRIPTURE DISCUSSION COMMENTARY 5

Series editor: Laurence Bright

Histories II

Hamish Swanston

Joshua

1 and 2 Chronicles

Ezra–Nehemiah

1 and 3 Maccabees

ACTA Foundation

Adult Catechetical Teaching Aids

Chicago, Illinois

First published 1972
ACTA Foundation (Adult Catechetical Teaching Aids),
4848 N. Clark Street, Chicago, Illinois 60640

Nihil obstat : John M. T. Barton STD LSS   *Censor*
Imprimatur : + Victor Guazzelli   *Vicar General*
Westminster, 29 December 1971

2542

Library of Congress Catalog number 71–173033

ISBN 0 87946 004 0

Made and printed in Great Britain by
William Clowes & Sons, Limited
London, Beccles and Colchester

Contents

General Introduction *Laurence Bright*   vii

Introduction to the later histories *Hamish*
Swanston   1

Book list   20

Joshua   23

1 Entering the land *Jos 1 : 1–5 : 12*   25
2 The first campaign *Jos 5 : 13–8 : 35*   33
3 The conquest *Jos 9 : 1–12 : 24*   41
4 Settlements *Jos 13 : 1–22 : 34*   49
5 Covenant liturgy *Jos 23 : 1–24 : 33*   57

1 and 2 Chronicles   69

1 The setting for the temple and its liturgy
     1 Chron 1 : 1–16 : 43   71
2 The temple—preparations *1 Chron 17 : 1–22 : 19*   83
3 The temple—completion *1 Chron 23 : 1–2*
     Chron 9 : 31   95
4 A succession of kings *2 Chron 10 : 1–28 : 27*   109
5 The end of the line *2 Chron 29 : 1–36 : 23*   126

Ezra and Nehemiah   139

1 The edict of Cyrus *Ez 1 : 1–6 : 22*   141
2 Nehemiah the governor *Neh 1 : 1–6 : 14;*
     12 : 1–13 : 30; 10 : 1–39   151
3 The assembly *Neh 6 : 15–7 : 73; 11 : 1–36;*
     Ez 7 : 1–10 : 44; Neh 9 : 1–38; 8 : 1–18   160

Contents

1 Maccabees   169

Introduction   171
1   Mattathias *1 Mac 1:1–2:70*   174
2   Judas *1 Mac 3:1–9:22*   182
3   Jonathan *1 Mac 9:23–12:53*   192
4   Simon *1 Mac 13:1–16:24*   198

2 Maccabees   201

Introduction   203
1   Letters and preface *2 Mac 1:1–2:32*   205
2   Stories, edifying and tall *2 Mac 3:1–15:39*   209

General Introduction

A few of the individual units which make up this series of biblical commentaries have already proved their worth issued as separate booklets. Together with many others they are now grouped together in a set of twelve volumes covering almost all the books of the old and new testaments—a few have been omitted as unsuitable to the general purpose of the series.

That purpose is primarily to promote discussion. This is how these commentaries differ from the others that exist. They do not cover all that could be said about the biblical text, but concentrate on the features most likely to get lively conversation going—those, for instance, with special relevance for later developments of thought, or for life in the church and world of today. For this reason passages of narrative are punctuated by sets of questions designed to get a group talking, though the text of scripture, helped by the remarks of the commentator, should have already done just that.

For the text is what matters. Individuals getting ready for a meeting, the group itself as it meets, should always have the bible centrally present, and use the commentary only as a tool. The bibliographies will help those wishing to dig deeper.

What kinds of group can expect to work in this way?

Absolutely any. The bible has the reputation of being difficult, and in some respects it is, but practice quickly clears up a lot of initial obstacles. So parish groups of any kind can and should be working on it. The groups needn't necessarily already exist, it is enough to have a few like-minded friends and to care sufficiently about finding out what the bible means. Nor need they be very large; one family could be quite enough. High schools (particularly in the senior year), colleges and universities are also obvious places for groups to form. If possible they should everywhere be ecumenical in composition: though all authors are Roman catholics, there is nothing sectarian in their approach.

In each volume there are two to four or occasionally more studies of related biblical books. Each one is self-contained; it is neither necessary nor desirable to start at the beginning and plough steadily through. Take up, each time, what most interests you—there is very little in scripture that is actually dull! Since the commentaries are by different authors, you will discover differences of outlook, in itself a matter for discussion. Above all, remember that getting the right general approach to reading the bible is more important than answering any particular question about the text—and that this approach only comes with practice.

Volume 5 contains the post-exilic Chronicler's history, which includes Ezra–Nehemiah, preceded by Joshua, which was one of its models. The two books of Maccabees, from the second century BC, represent the final stage of Israel's history-writing.

LAURENCE BRIGHT

Introduction to the later histories

Originally 1 and 2 Chronicles formed the one collection, *dibre hayyamim*, the records of the days. Such official annals were kept by most Near Eastern courts. Esther refers to the chronicles of the kings of Media and Persia, and it is evident that both northern and southern Hebrew kingdoms followed the pagan example in this matter.

Originally, too, Chronicles led into the first versions of Ezra–Nehemiah, but Ezra was employed as a supplement to Samuel and Kings, so its beginning was filled out a little from Chronicles material. Hence the obvious overlapping in the present texts. When Chronicles came into the canon later and was placed between Kings and Ezra no one bothered to remove the passages inserted at the beginning of Ezra and we have the uncomfortable duplication still. This prevents a continuous reading of Chronicles and Ezra–Nehemiah and so disguises their original shape.

Their author certainly did not care to compose for his chosen period a great historical narrative comparable to the magnificent effort of those who put together the Deuteronomic history of the nation. The Chronicler intended rather to produce a work which would enable his contemporaries to look at their present condition with a special form of understanding.

The Deuteronomist had worked that his readers might appreciate the activity of the word of the Lord in their history, and to bring them to hope for a realisation of a new Davidic kingdom. The exile in Babylon becomes, in the final version of the Deuteronomist's history, a warning of how things would go if the nation did not obey the word of the Lord. The release of Jehoiachin (2 Kg 25 : 27–30) may be a sign of how the nation may yet prosper.

The Deuteronomist's warning was evidently not effective in bringing the nation to appreciate its own condition as servant of Yahweh. The Chronicler felt a demand being made upon him to do something in the new situation. Just as the deportations of 721 and the submission of Ahaz to Assyria had brought the southern Yahwists to recognise a vocation to spread the good news of Yahweh among their unfortunate northern brethren, so the events of 587 and the exile suggested to the Chronicler a vocation to speak again of the significance of the southern disaster.

Joshua

The Chronicler had a multitude of sources for his work, official records like 'the book of the chronicles of King David' (1 Chron 27 : 24), the scribal comments on 'the chronicle of the kings' (2 Chron 24 : 27) and the text of Solomon's decree (2 Chron 25 : 4), genealogical lists from official records (1 Chron 4 : 33, 9 : 22 etc), records of various seers kept by their disciples (1 Chron 29 : 29, 2 Chron 9 : 29, 20 : 34, 33 : 19), copies of royal letters from the court archives (2 Chron 32 : 10 ff) and of priestly documents from the temple archives (1 Chron 28 : 19), as well as the great deuteronomistic history, the liturgical service books (2 Chron 29:30) and Lamentations (2 Chron 35:25). These provided his material. It seems likely that the book of Joshua provided him with the interpretative principles for the presentation of this material as meaningful for his contemporaries.

By 515 the second temple was complete, the Davidic line had ceased to be politically effective, and the way was clear for a new society, centred on the cultic celebration of the covenant, to flourish in Judah. But things went wrong. The new community envisaged by Haggai and Zephaniah was already starting towards the disintegration described in Malachi.

Joel refers to plagues and drought (1:2 ff), Malachi speaks of border wars with Edom and the Arabs (1:2–4), and both lament the religious lethargy of the people and the indifference of the priests (Jl 2:12 f, Mal 1:6–14, 2:1–9). The Chronicler, looking at this situation, subjects all such economic, political and cultural explanations of Judah's condition to the chief cause that he finds in the religious opposition of the men who had taken over the land during the exile, and who would not yield to the Israelites now returning (cf Hag 2:14 and Ezra 4:4–5). There had to be a restoration of the old Israelite purity.

Inter-marriage between the impure people of the country and Yahweh's own men, even the levites, (Ezra 10:18–44, Neh 10:30), was having effects similar to those of Solomon's earlier marriages of that kind. The culture of the community was polluted by pagan practices and fashions (Neh 13:26). Stern measures in the name of the mosaic law were demanded if the land was to be made pure again. And these were put into effect first by Nehemiah and then, more forcefully, by Ezra. Racial purity came to be recognised as the only way to protect religious orthodoxy and cultural unity. The demand of the reformers was for a racial, tribal Israelitism, militantly opposed to the contaminating influences of the alien inhabitants of the land. It was of such a demand and an effective response to it that the Chronicler and his fellows read in Joshua.

Joshua spoke to their condition at three significant moments:

(1) *Concerning the leader*

Nehemiah's authority derived not from kingly lineage nor from direct divine vocation, and it could therefore be challenged by all kinds of unhelpful elements in Jerusalem. The historic authority of Joshua offered an example of how a man might truly be doing the work of Yahweh without formal appointment in either of these ways.

(2) *Concerning the land*

The returning exiles knew that the Palestinian land belonged by right to them but they were not safely installed, they had still to dispossess the aliens who had been settled in Samaria by the pagan authorities. The story of Joshua's conquest of the land showed that Yahweh's forces could gain control of the land Yahweh had given them despite the strength of pagan opposition.

(3) *Concerning the people*

The great danger to pure Yahwism in the new community came from association with the foreigner and his idolatries. The marching column of returning exiles must be kept from the lures of the country folk, and the history of Joshua's campaign through Palestine showed how he dealt with such a situation and kept Israel pure.

The people were to become again 'the congregation' they had been with Joshua. There are twenty-two refer-

ences in the Chronicler's work to this 'congregation of
Israel (the *qahal*) while this religious description of the
people occurs only four times in 1 and 2 Kings. This
statistic, at the least, is significant of an effort to return
to the Joshua way of covenant life. Joshua is presented
here, therefore, as that book of the old histories which
most probably excited the Chronicler to an appreciation
of the meaning of his own times, and offered him a suggestion for dealing with the difficulties of those times.

It is not clear just how old a history was the written
form of the Joshua traditions when the Chronicler set to
work on his own account of Israel. That Joshua is written
rather later that the events it recounts is quickly shown.
Institutions and conditions, like the twelve stones at the
Jordan crossing (4:9), the name of Gilgal (5:9), the
family of Rahab (6:25), are said to be continuing 'to this
day', which implies some lengthy history. But how long
is that history?

The iron vessels of 6:19 and 6:24 demonstrate that
the writer lived at a time somewhat later than the 13th
century, for iron was not used at all commonly in Israel
until after 1200. And the historian declares that he has
used sources which belong to the period of the monarchy;
the poem, for example, at Bibeon (10:13) comes from the
Book of Jashar, which at 2 Sam 1:17 f is said to have
contained David's lament for Saul, so this brings us down
to the period of the second king of Israel. The writer
seems also to know about the temple complex, its treasury
(6:19), its altar (9:27) and its Cisjordan site (22:19). The
oath at Jericho (6:26) is a prophecy after the event of the
incident in 1 Kg 16:35 and so puts the composition of
this version of the book into the mid-ninth century at
least. A later date of composition still can be put for
23:12–13, and perhaps the whole book, for this seems to

be written with a knowledge of the exile, but not perhaps of the return.

At any rate the Chronicler found Joshua to be his kind of history. The book dealt with matters that concerned him, and dealt with them in ways he understood.

The Chronicler

It has been a commonplace of old testament criticism that while we may profitably spend time considering the Deuteronomist's work as a proper piece of history writing and measuring his account of the past of Israel against the standards we use for Herodotus and Acton, the Chronicler was so far from understanding the historian's business that we cannot find a place to start reading his work as a history. There seems nowhere we might begin to correct him by the facts. This is customarily regarded not as a piece of brilliant escapology on the part of the Chronicler, but as a sad sign of what religion can do to a man if it once takes a grip on his scholarship.

But the Chronicler did have a view of the historian's vocation. And he worked with this in mind. The Chronicler's view is the fairly common one that the present reality reveals what the past must have been like. If we look carefully enough at the present then we shall find out the character of the past that led into this present. The distinction of the Chronicler from most others who hold this simple notion is that he believes that the present reveals the past in a quite straightforward way. He does not think that the present makes explicit what was implicit in the past. He thinks that things must always have been as they are now.

The generality of men may fall sometimes into talk of 'human nature' and their not being able to change it.

They may enjoy psychological anachronisms in tales of Henry VIII or Elizabeth I as television presents them in a readily understandable complex of customary motives. But they do not generally suppose that the law courts and the drainage of the past were conducted in quite the same way as they are today—and this despite the evidence of fanciful wigs and gowns in the present law courts and the splendid water-pipes at Knossos. We allow that men may be the same under the skin whatever the pageant costume, though we rejoice in a sense of history which says that things are always changing.

The Chronicler in order that his main themes should not be missed pays no attention to historical detail. He writes as if everything in the first temple, for example, was the model for the corresponding thing in the post-exilic temple he knew. This allows him to devote attention to the elucidation of the unalterable significance of the worship men offer in the temple.

It is difficult for us at this separated time to appreciate that the Chronicler is not making a series of historical mistakes that we, with our knowledge of Egyptian and Assyrian archives and our digs into Canaanite mounds, can correct. He was not making mistakes, he was rather deliberately putting the history into modern dress for precisely those reasons which prompt Dr Miller to stage the *Merchant of Venice* in nineteenth-century costume and Mr Brooke to play *A Midsummer Night's Dream* as a circus. He wants to bring out the significance of the action of history.

The making clear of meanings was for the Chronicler the proper work of the historian. The historian performed the function of the levite for the community at large. The levite explained the meaning of events, festivals and old prophecies to the little community within which he served. The historian, as the Chronicler under-stood his function, explained history to the whole com-munity of Israel.

It may be that the Chronicler was himself a member of the Jerusalem levitical group. It is noticeable from even a cursory reading of his history how greatly he admired this order of men. They appear so much more frequently in his work than in the Deuteronomist's code and narrative. Something at least must be said of the levites if the Chronicler is to be understood.

The levites

The origin of the levites is a much disputed matter. The etymology of *Levi* has been traced to 'a whirling dance', 'a man attached', and a verb meaning 'to give as a pledge', and so theories of levite origins have been concerned with dervish dances, with men being attached to Yahweh, and with men being given over, consecrated, to Yahweh's use. None of these three notions can be properly substantiated. Num 18:2–4 suggests that the levites were 'attached' to Aaron, and 1 Sam 1:28 describes the little boy being 'given over' to Yahweh, so both of these theories have some scriptural backing, but I like best the arbitrary notion of the respectable levites deriving from the wild men of the camp. They were later so sensible and staid that it is nice to think of them as once like the leaping priests of Baal or the juggler of Notre Dame.

The work of the levites was originally to carry the ark as it journeyed with the wandering Jews, and to look after the ark when it was put down in the camp. On the final settlement of the ark in Jerusalem the levites remained with their charge in the new sanctuary and assisted the senior priests in the preparation and action of the liturgy.

They gradually assumed a central importance in the cult and became in many matters quite indistinguishable from the Aaronite and Zadokite priests.

The Chronicler has included certain old records of the levitical activities in the days of Nehemiah and Ezra, and it can be safely asserted that three families of levites came to Jerusalem from Babylon with Nehemiah (Neh 7 : 43) and two other families with Ezra (Ezra 2.40), but since the names of levites mentioned in other parts of the narrative certainly come from other families than these, it must be assumed that the returning levites married into families, whether originally levitical or not is discussable, who had remained in Judah during the Persian occupation. This suggests that conservatism, at least in the matter of blood, grew up between the time of Nehemiah and Ezra and that of the Chronicler. For the Chronicler certainly intended to keep the levitical strain pure from all contaminating blood like that of those who had not gone into exile. Those who remained in Judah had been content to allow all kinds of syncretist cults to be performed in the hill sanctuaries. The land had been polluted by the nastiest pagan rituals. Those who could live in a country while this was going on were totally unfit, in the Chronicler's eyes, to marry good Jews who had kept themselves pure from contamination in the Persian capital. He read back his conservative regulations into the earlier period of the return.

In Nehemiah's and Ezra's time the sanctuary levites were distinguished from both the singers and the gate-keepers, but either in the Chronicler's own time or that of his later editor, the three groups were lumped together as levites. This had the effect of increasing the numbers of levites, since everybody had been promoted upwards, and of giving them a greater say in the shaping of society.

It may be that as an effort against these late pretensions some priestly writer invented the story of Korah (Num 16) where the levites are put in a very unfavourable light and accused of usurping the office, functions and privileges of the Aaronite priests. A reply to the kind of priestly criticism that this story represents can be read in the levitical Book of Jubilees.

And, considering how important clergy have always thought vestments to be, the moment of greatest levitical triumph may have been when the representatives of the levitical groups persuaded Agrippa II to grant them the right to wear linen vestments like the old priests.

The Chronicler emphasises the levitical ministry at every point and thus answers a question of some importance for his community: On whom can the orthodox rely for the continuance of the renewal movement in Jerusalem? Obviously they could not rely on the laymen who would entertain Sabbath traders and Moabite wives if they were left to their own devices for a moment. Nor could they rely on the priests, Aaronite or Zadokite, for they too, more surprisingly perhaps, were fascinated by the foreign girls, and in Nehemiah's time it was the high priest himself who gave a syncretist heretic rooms in the temple itself. The only men the Chronicler could trust were the levites. These, on their missionary journeys preaching the law, and in their devotion to the details of the ritual, have declared themselves to be faithful advocates of the reform.

The levites must be encouraged. The Chronicler makes great play with the genealogies of the levitical families. In 1 Chron 6, for example, the office as the Chronicler knew it is read back by blood to the unknowable past. In 1 Chron 15–16, what might be thought to be a description of the last service required of the levites, who were ordained only to carry the ark, becomes an account of the levites being invested with new temple responsibilities, and this investiture is elaborated at 1 Chron 23:1–32.

The teaching ministry of the levites is first mentioned in the Deuteronomist's work, but the references there may not be part of the original text, and probably do not antedate the Chronicler's account of Jehoshaphat's encouragement of their teaching ministry (2 Chron 17:7–9). At any rate the Chronicler is the levites' historian. He intends that those who are promoting orthodoxy in the community should be held in high respect.

The great scene when Ezra reads the law, or selections from it, and the people suddenly realise their need to enter into obedience before Yahweh, is described by the Chronicler in such a way that the levites are recognised as Ezra's left and right hand men. The levites are the ones who make the law understandable of the people by first translating the Hebrew reading into Aramaic and then explaining the meaning of Yahweh's grace.

The influence of the levitical missions and the homiletic style of their instruction of the Judah people can be observed directly in several of the speeches attributed to seers and statesmen in the narrative. These incidental reflections are noted in the body of these comments on the text. And, most importantly, one may descry in the whole structure and manner of the Chronicler's work the traits of the levitical sermon and its didactic interests. The Chronicler, like any village levite, knows that it is important to moralise enthusiastically on the law's demands, the consecration of the people by the sabbath rest, the redemption from sin offered in the cult, and the revelation of history's meaning at the celebration of the glorious feast of Tabernacles.

A Davidic messianism?

Generally the commentators on the Chronicler's work have remarked what they take to be his intense devotion to the house of David, and many have seen in this an indication of the Chronicler's messianic hope for a coming man who will put all things right.

Certainly there is a good deal in 1 and 2 Chronicles about David and his successors on the throne of Judah, as one might expect in an account of the events of the nation's history at this time, particularly an account written in Jerusalem, the city of David, when it was struggling to become again the centre of a Jewish community.

But the theory of the Chronicler as a man who saw the Davidic line as the way in which Yahweh would bring about a restoration of Israel's glory becomes more difficult to sustain when the accounts of Nehemiah and Ezra, evidently the work of the same author as Chronicles, are under discussion. For here there is nothing, not even at Ezra 9:7–9 or Neh 9:36, to substantiate a Davidic theory. Those who would maintain that the Chronicler put great hopes upon the Davidic line are driven to assume that the silence of the Chronicler in his later work concerning Davidic messianism is to be explained by the political conditions of foreign domination under which the Chronicler was working. A gentile government would be unlikely, the theory goes, to permit the dissemination of propaganda for a coming leader of the Jews.

Well, this may be the explanation. But the argument rests upon a silence which, like many another silence, can be interpreted quite differently. 1 and 2 Chronicles seem to me to be concerned with David and the kings of Judah not because there is something sacred in the line but because this line of kings for a while carried on the sacred task of leading the covenant community. The covenant with Abraham shapes the character of Israel's history and is given great prominence by the Chronicler (cf, for example, 1 Chron 16 : 16 ff). It is precisely because the covenant itself, and not the transient ministers of the covenant, occupies first place in the Chronicler's esteem that he does not spend time talking of Moses or Joshua or the judges of the past, and that he speaks of the Davidic line only when it is through the means of that family that the covenant is projected into the future. When the royal house is virtually extinct he does not spend time looking around for another Davidic prince, though he could have found one, nor does he set to work on making secret affirmation of messianism through David in such a way that the Persians will not discover his meaning. He gets on with the job of demonstrating that the covenant made by Yahweh with Abraham and his people for ever is made present through other means. He points out the covenant continuance through the work of the governor appointed by the foreigner and the first high priest of the second temple.

The Chronicler is neither an antiquarian nor a seer. He is simply a man whose faith is not tied to any individual manifestation of Yahweh's love, but rather rests in the amazing fact that the covenant can be maintained in the community despite the extraordinary changes made in its historical circumstances. The Chronicler's messianism is certainly decipherable. It is to be read in 1 and 2 Chronicles and in Ezra–Nehemiah. It is a popular messianism which looks for an eternal history of Yahweh's love for Israel. Nothing in the future, however odd the events may prove, just as nothing in the past, not Egyptian domination, nor Canaanite fertility dances, nor Mesopotamian imperialism, will be able to put an end to the vocation begun when Abraham was called to be the friend of Yahweh.

The exile

At the first deportation of 597 only the most distinguished citizens of Jerusalem and the country towns of Judah were taken to Babylon. The book of Jeremiah tells us quite a deal about conditions of Jerusalem for the next decade and should be read as background material to the study of these post-exilic narratives.

Then in 587, and again after the murder of Gedaliah (2 Kg 25 : 22 ff), further deportations of lesser men were ordered by the occupying power. This left the city with few men who could organise Jewish corporate life. After the first deportation, Jeremiah had continued his efforts to recall the people to the service of Yahweh, but now the combination of his political opposition to the authorities and his contempt for the ecclesiastics who were in charge of the temple cult, led only to his being at first locked up by the ruling party, and then carried off forcibly to Egypt with those whose plots came to a futile climax with the assassination of Gedaliah. Jeremiah had, perhaps, looked forward to a day when men might approach Yahweh without the fuss of the ritual any more. And he may have had just this happiness during his last days in Egypt.

It seems that the Jews who fled to Egypt and settled at Daphnae and Elephantine reached an unholy accommodation with their neighbours and lapsed into syncretist nonsenses. They were at any rate not counted by the Jerusalem men as being true Jews any more.

Those great men of the nation who had not been caught up in the Babylonian deportations had fled with Johanan to Egypt. The state of Jerusalem and Judah revealed in

Lamentations is a sorry one. This book is probably a compilation of fragments from the sad liturgies recited round the makeshift altar among the temple ruins. The liturgy of this remnant lacked, of course, priestly and levitical legitimacy, and could not be accepted by the orthodox as the proper cultic act of Judah. This was particularly the case after the assassination of Gedaliah, when the Jerusalem cult like the rest of Jewish society came under the jurisdiction of the Persian governor of Samaria and was thus incurably tainted.

On the other hand the prayer-meetings of those in Babylon by the Chebar canal gave little sense of Yahweh's presence among his people. The Jews did not yet understand that Yahweh was with them wherever they were. So, despite their prosperity in the alien capital, a number of these exiles looked for an opportunity to return to Jerusalem and to renew the true liturgy. They formed the new conservative party. Among these Babylonian exiles Ezekiel set up little house-groups which met for the study of the law of Moses. To these the one religious institution left was the sabbath and the one racial distinction was that of circumcision. They made much of them, and thus began a tradition of huge reverence for these aspects of Jewish life.

The dream of Ezekiel was of a community that would be composed of men responsible to their consciences for a better future and not held in fear of corporate guilt for the past. His community would be presided over by the priest of Zadok's line with a lay prince to look after material government, particularly the support of the liturgy. In this community all would be clean. The foreigner and the ritually impure would be refused a place in the pilgrimage procession of the revitalised tribes as they went singing to the new temple.

The Chronicler does not name Ezekiel in his work but this vision of the new society seems to have influenced greatly the character of his history. He has chosen to describe the return from the exile as a gradual preparation for the celebration of the liturgy in the new temple. The return is a cultic procession and the Chronicler is not willing to waste much space on the great events of imperial politics which made the procession possible. Yahweh managed all when the people were ready to take part as clean members of his community.

The return was made possible historically by changes in the structure of Mesopotamian power. Babylon was not a secure and stable power. On 29 October 539 the last Babylonian king, Nabonidus, was deposed by the conquering Cyrus. The Achaemenid Cyrus had become leader of the Medes at Ecbatana, defeated the legendary Croesus in 546, and after 539 was the ruler of the whole Near East except Egypt, which fell later to his son Cambyses. These military events made possible a new lease of liturgical life for the Jews in Jerusalem.

The old Babylonian policy of keeping peoples subject by deportations which placed them in unfamiliar surroundings was reversed. All over the empire men began to pack in readiness to return home. All over the empire the guardians of local shrines began to collect timbers and incense when it was learnt that Cyrus had decreed that local languages and cults should be allowed within the imperial boundaries and even be acknowledged as part of the official life of the Persian empire. Cyrus took upon himself the responsibility which had belonged to all the old local rulers in their pettydoms before the imperial armies had sent them scurrying, and one of these responsibilities was the upkeep of the local shrines. And among these shrines, not distinguished in Cyrus' mind from many another tribal high place, was the temple of Jerusalem. Cyrus agreed to finance the reconstruction of the royal shrine of the kings of Judah. He appointed a Babylonian official to see to all the necessary arrangements. But here the matter stayed. Sheshbazzar, like many another civil servant, was not in a hurry to get things going. The shrine at Jerusalem was perhaps inspected but no builders or carpenters arrived to do the work, and no money seems to have reached Jerusalem to pay for the reconstruction.

Among the exiles Jewish prophetic activity reached its climax with the work of the second Isaiah, a man whose name is unknown to us and whose work is inserted at various places in Isaiah, so that it was for some time generally thought to be the work of the pre-exilic counsellor of King Ahaz. Certain elements in the work however demonstrate to any sane man's satisfaction that parts of the book were written among the exiles. This second Isaiah comforted his fellows in Babylon with a proclamation of Yahweh as universal ruler, the Lord of history, who would in the end, if only they would measure up to their responsibilities as members of the covenant community, bring about the happiness of all descendants of Abraham.

The exile and the return were interpreted by second Isaiah as a renewal of the exodus redemption, leading to a splendid time of grace and prosperity. It was therefore possible for this intelligent seer to accept as inevitable the passing of the Davidic kings. Incidents like the reigns of David and Cyrus are moments in the grand march of Yahweh's people through history. This was an important idea. It enabled the Jews to break with some restrictions upon their self-appreciation. It allowed the people to prepare themselves for a new thing, a realisation of the covenant community in a new way, passing through a time in Jerusalem of Persian governors and high priests to an universal reign of Yahweh.

The Second Isaiah's constant belief in Yahweh's working out the redemption of Israel as a people, is reflected in the opening chapters of the Chronicler's history. The genealogies provided a tribal and familial context for events at Jerusalem, making of those events the centre of a universal history for all tribes and families, a history which does not depend for its vitality on any king.

Ezra–Nehemiah

Israelite discussion of any historical incident or period has generally this shape:

(a) Yahweh gives a benefit to men
(b) Yahweh imposes a precept
(c) Man rebels
(d) Yahweh punishes the rebellion
(e) Yahweh reconciles man to himself

We can see such a shape at work in the account of Adam in Genesis:

(a) Adam is created and given a garden of trees and animals
(b) A command is given that he is not to eat the fruit of one tree
(c) He disobeys the command
(d) Adam loses the garden and its happiness
(e) A promise is made that the punishment will be brought to an end

We can see the shape, too, in the story of the exodus:

(a) The Israelites are brought out of Egypt by Yahweh
(b) Yahweh imposes the law at Sinai

(c) The Israelites grouse and grumble and bow down before the 'golden calf'
(d) The levitical massacre
(e) The renewal of the covenant.

What distinguishes the Chronicler from the other Israelite historians is his belief that the liturgy offers his contemporaries a way into grace. For him the structure of history for the individual and for the whole people has been given a liturgical interpretation. We now ought to read history something like this:

(a) Yahweh bestows grace
(b) Yahweh imposes a precept
(c) Man sins
(d) Catastrophe comes down on him
(e) Reconciliation takes place within the celebration of the liturgy of penance and forgiveness.

The final section of 2 Chronicles is based upon a structure of the king's recognition of sin, an act of penance, a return to the acknowledgement of the covenant as determining the character of Israelite life, and a celebration of the liturgy.

This is also the structure of Ezra–Nehemiah. The book, whatever its value as an historical record of the first days of the post-exilic community (and this is, in fact, considerable) is interesting as giving the realisation in community life of the individual conversion of the king described at the end of Chronicles. The community life, which is, after all, the real interest of the Chronicler, is described in Ezra–Nehemiah as a movement from the recognition of sin, through penance, and an acknowledgement of the law, to the celebration of the Jerusalem liturgy.

In the notes on Ezra–Nehemiah attention will be concentrated on this movement. Little will be said of the peculiar difficulties of textual criticism, and nothing at all of the many arguments about historical conundrums in the narrative. It will be assumed simply that the generally accepted disorder of the sections should, on this ideological basis, be organised into the following sequence:

I   Cyrus' Edict and the first return from the Babylonian Exile (Ezra 1–6)

II The coming of Nehemiah from Artaxerxes' court and the rebuilding of the walls (Neh 1–6:14 and 12:1–13:31 and 10:1 ff)

III The coming of Ezra and the performance of the liturgy (Neh 6:15–7:72a and 11:1 ff; Ezra 7:1–8:23; Neh 9 and 8, and Ezra 10).

Introductory notices for 1 and 2 Maccabees are placed at the beginning of the commentaries on these two books, for they do not belong with the body of work associated with the Chronicler. They are later interpretations of Israel's history and develop in ways appropriate to their later times the Chronicler's understanding of event and liturgy.

Booklist

There are far too few commentaries of a generally-usable kind on the material considered in this volume. C. F. Burney's commentary on Judges, though published in 1930, is still interesting, but it needs to be supplemented by a reading of John Bright's commentary in the 'Interpreter's Bible', Volume II, (New York, 1953). Together with Professor Jacob Myer's three volumes in the 'Anchor Bible' series on 1 and 2 Chronicles and Ezra and Nehemiah, which are often most helpful, the reader should consult the sections devoted to the Chronicler's work in the revised edition of Peake's *Commentary*, and may find those in the *New Catholic Commentary on Holy Scripture* interesting on particular matters.

For 1 and 2 Maccabees the required background information may be had from D. S. Russell's lively little book *The Jews from Alexander to Herod*, and the relevant sections of the 'Interpreter's Bible'.

HAMISH SWANSTON

Joshua

1

Entering the land
Jos 1:1–5:12

Jos 1

Joshua ('Yahweh is salvation', Num 13:16, and Hebrew
for 'Jesus'), originally named Hoshea ('he saves', Num
13:8), is presented in the history as the chosen successor
of Moses because of his close association with the great
man in the latter part of the exodus journey. Moses'
personal relationship with Joshua may have been a construction of the Israelite story-teller but the importance
of Joshua is not his relation to any man but his continuing faith in Yahweh's power and promise, and his service
of Yahweh for the salvation of the people.

Despite his interest in Moses the historian knows that
the true centre of his work is precisely that continuance
of Yahweh's care which is made manifest in the work of
this second man. So the historian gets straight on with
the preliminary announcement of Moses' death and its
immediate follow-up: 'Rise, it is time'.

It is time for the Israelites to be given the promised
land—a land whose limits were to be the Lebanon moun-
tains to the north, the desert in the south, the Euphrates
on the east, and the seacoast on the west. These ideal
boundaries were never reached, but the Israelites were
always hoping for such a huge territory, and expecting
it to be realised soon—one of the holds Solomon had over

the people, despite his ferociously oppressive domestic policies, was the nearness that his foreign policy brought them to achieving their grandiose territorial ambitions.

The land is the land of promise. The condition of possession is, therefore, that the people maintain their allegiance to the covenant. The law is paramount. And the historian is happy to read back into the primitive time he is describing a fully codified law like that which he himself had been taught to obey.

The first verses of the book of Joshua are dominated, too, by the historian's sense of Yahweh's presence among his people. Yahweh is with them at all times. The death of the leader affects the relationship that Yahweh has with the whole people not at all. Perhaps, since there is no reference to any religious place in these verses, no shrine as the setting for Joshua's commission, there is an indication here of the historian's appreciation of Yahweh as not requiring a tabernacle, a city or a temple, in order to be present. If so, then it might indicate, with 23 : 13, a date for the composition of the book during the exile before the return to Jerusalem and the consequent emphasis on the importance of rebuilding.

The emphasis in 1 : 10 ff is upon an ordered entry of those who rightfully own the land and expect to possess it. The notion of having to fight to conquer someone else's territory is not allowed to intrude upon this happy sense of ownership.

The conquest is declared, by the demand that the Transjordan tribes assist at the crossing, to be a national concern. In Judges each tribe is shown fighting for its own future and sometimes the tribes are represented as fighting each other. This is unthinkable to the Joshua historian. The whole Israelite nation takes the whole land as a nation and then the national territory is divided among the participatory tribes.

The historian of Judges evidently had it in mind to demonstrate the need for a king to unite the people. He has Davidic matters in view. The Joshua historian is assured of national unity because of Yahweh's presence and promise. He is not convinced of the necessity of a king.

Jos 2

The spies that Joshua sends into Jericho are said by the men of the city to be reconnoitring the whole country. The area is to be conquered at one blow. Rahab herself is somehow aware of Yahweh's will for the Israelites. They are going to be given everything, and she, a citizen of the place, is not only not a traitress (for she serves the true owners of the city) but has to ask the Israelites to allow her to go on living in Jericho. Joshua's assessment, 2:24, is one of the conquest being already accomplished. Everyone, Israelite and Canaanite, friend and enemy, acknowledges Yahweh's gift of the country to his people.

Jos 3–4

The conquest, therefore, is not to be one of savage and dangerous battles. The Israelites are not to risk their lives for their land. It is a free gift. The whole story of the capture of Jericho is related as a religious ceremony. The levites raise the ark of the covenant on their shoulders and move to the head of the ritual procession of Israel, the people follow at the prescribed reverential distance, having purified themselves for the cultic act, obeying the ritual demands of a later age. The procession moves off to the Jordan river and, as at the Reed Sea, does not stop when it comes to the water's edge. The waters stop when they reach the procession, just as they were later thought to have stood at the Reed Sea crossing. The Metro-Goldwyn-Mayer version of the Reed Sea event is due to an ancient, very ancient, misreading of the records, and has evidently influenced the historian in his construction of the Jordan narrative here.

There is absolutely no justification for allowing our literal selves the luxury of comparing the Jordan crossing of the Israelites, around 1200 BC or so, with the 1267, 1909 or 1927 collapses of the river bank which each dammed up the river and made it possible to cross dryshod. Such things would only distract the modern reader from the historian's purpose in composing the narrative. He wants the reader to see the wonder not as a physical accident or coincidence, but as a sign of Yahweh's powerful presence with his people for an event which he has arranged carefully. The slow passing of the ark of Yahweh, not some heap of bank-rubble, holds back the river, and no one in 1267, 1909 or 1927 beheld the lower waters stop running to the sea.

3 : 12 has to be taken with 4 : 2 f. The tribes set up the stones to mark the place where Yahweh acted. But the stones are not merely markers. They are signs of the power of Yahweh and share something of his holiness. The twelve stones became sacred themselves, like the stones that Gilgamesh strikes in a profane manner on the way to the waters surrounding the home of his immortal grandfather. That the holiness of the twelve stones came at last to occupy a place in local superstition can be discerned from this account.

The first version of the crossing story evidently stated that the stones were taken from the river bed and set up

at the first stopping place of the procession this side of
the Jordan. There must have grown up some ceremonial
remembrance of the crossing, and verses 6 and 7 are perhaps part of the stone-liturgy. The question and answer
beginning to a Jewish ceremony appears, of course, most
significantly in the passover ritual when the young boy
is required even now to ask the president of the meal
'What is the meaning of this?' (cf Ex 12:26, 13:14, and
Deut 6:20, 29:22). 4:8 is simply the record of Joshua
setting up the stones in the camp, but at 4:9 there is a
sudden change in the telling of the story. It is evidently
an insertion made by some orthodox scribe to counter
idolatries at Gilgal. The stones are now said to be placed
in the river bed and are therefore quite out of reach and
sight. Therefore it is impossible for any cult to be celebrated round the stones. The scribe intends to kill the
cult of the men at Gilgal by declaring that whatever they
have thought they were doing they were in fact rever-
encing stones with no sacred significance at all.

4:19–24 provides a repetition of the original story and
the justification for the Gilgal cult. Perhaps it was
thought necessary to add these verses lest 4:6 f had been
cancelled out by 4:9. The principle at work in the
various revisions of the text by later scribes of whatever
sentiment is always to add more material rather than cut
out that which has already been accepted as part of the
holy record.

The procession passes across (4:10 ff) and everything
is done according to the arrangements outlined in chapter 1. The people enter Canaan on the same day of the
year that Ezekiel saw his first vision (cf Ezek 40:1). It may
have been a traditional day for the beginning of a holy
enterprise.

Gilgal

At Gilgal (which means 'stone circle', a name that was used of other places, cf Deut 11 : 30, 1 Kg 2 : 1), the stones are set up and the crossing of the Jordan explicitly likened to the crossing at the Sea of Reeds.

Gilgal, about two and a half miles from the river bank, became the chief shrine of the Benjamites. It was there that the people proclaimed Saul 'king before Yahweh' (1 Sam 11 : 15), and there too that Saul disobeyed Yahweh and performed the ritual sacrifice, bringing down a curse upon himself (1 Sam 13 : 7–14) and there he was rejected by Yahweh when Samuel came to slay Agag 'before Yahweh at Gilgal' (1 Sam 5 : 12 ff). Amos preached, later, against the immorality of worshippers at the shrine (Am 4 : 4) and prophesied its destruction (Am 5 : 5). Hosea thought the shrine so given to immoralities that to go on a pilgrimage to Gilgal was simply to play the whore's game of infidelity to Yahweh (Hos 4 : 15), and he located the beginning of all Israel's troubles at the place (Hos 9 : 15), in the end dismissing the shrine as the sanctuary where 'they sacrifice to bulls' (Hos 12 : 12).

1. Is it only our faith in an eternal God that prompts us to suppose that our present religious customs and beliefs represent an unalterable and age-old tradition?

2. Why do we delight in myths and yet engage in demythologising the tales which provide such fun?

Jos 5

While the country waits in terror for the coming of the Israelite army, Joshua makes it clear to his men that the Israelites are separated from all others. He circumcises the soldiers.

The Babylonians did not, it seems, use circumcision rites and probably the historian is thinking here of the way in which the men of Israel had used the rite to distinguish themselves from ,their overlords during the period of the exile. Certainly it would not have distinguished the Jews from their Canaanite neighbours at the time of Joshua since most of them employed circumcision in their puberty rituals.

Perhaps the 'Hill of Foreskins' was in later times the site of circumcision ceremonies connected with the Gilgal shrine and the whole story of Joshua's circumcision of the tribesmen before their entry upon their inheritance was an invention of the ministers of the Gilgal sanctuary who wished to give an added dignity to the place at a time when the story of the twelve stones was being attacked.

At any rate, whatever the origins of this part of the account, at the time of the historian's writing a man had to have been circumcised before he could take part in the celebrations of the passover, and since the historian was about to record the first passover in the holy land he needed a circumcision story at this point in his narrative. He certainly could not have provided an argument for the admission of the uncircumcised to the feast by omitting to specify the observance of the requirement in the days of antiquity.

Jos 5:12. The ceasing of the manna is the next sign that the old pilgrimage way of life is at an end. The Israelites are to settle down in their own farmsteads and live off the produce of their fields.

1. Should the first aim of an historian be to explain the shape of the present?

2. *Do we now approve of national rituals and insignia which proclaim the distinction of one group of men from another—does our standing at the playing of the national anthem have this kind of significance?*

3. *Why is it that cultic ceremonies customarily employ old-fashioned instruments, like Joshua's flint knife or our own candles?*

2

The first campaign
Jos 5:13–8:35

Jos 5:13–15. An angel opens the war

The sacred character of the military enterprise is manifest from the first sentence of the war-report. As Joshua stands in prayer before the investiture of Jericho the angelic commander of Yahweh's armies comes to him. Joshua lifts his eyes and sees the splendid warrior. He walks towards the angel with a challenge. The message of the angel has dropped out of the text. It may be that it is this message which is recapitulated in the angelic proclamation of Jg 2:1–2.

Yahweh is often called upon as *Yahweh Sebhaoth*, 'Lord of Armies', and this title may refer to Yahweh's command of the angelic hosts or, more probably, to Yahweh's command of Israel's armies. At this point in the narrative the military command is taken out of Joshua's hand and he is told, like Moses before the bush (Ex 3:5), to take off his shoes because the place has been made holy by the angelic presence. There is no evidence for the Israelites having in later years to take off their shoes before going into the temple, so the notion of discalcing must be remembered from a previous way of life. It is characteristic of course of the way of Islam which perhaps retains, here as elsewhere in its religious manners, desert customs.

33

Jos 6:1. From the theophany we pass to the liturgy. Jericho is shut up, it is as if it had been placed within a fairy-ring. Nothing can move in or out until the ritual has been completed. The warriors of Israel become temple servants marching each day round the town in procession, and we are given a sequence of magic numbers, seven priests, seven trumpets, seven days and seven circumambulations.

It is evident that the tale of Jericho as told by the historian has been patient of some rewriting by a later priestly scribe. Originally the tale was of Yahweh as the gatherer of military power, and the fall of Jericho took place after the soldiers had marched round the town on the seventh day. It was a military horn-blast that signalled the fall of the town walls. The version we have now results from a clerical editing. In our present text the levites are brought in to carry the ark round Jericho. The levites do not displace the warriors (we have seen in the story of the Gilgal stones that the scribes' custom was to lengthen uncomfortable texts until they said the right thing) but join in the procession.

Jos 6:6. Joshua is now said to give instructions to the priests before he orders the military arrangements, and the ark becomes the centre of a long procession of Israel, preceded by the guard of warriors, heralded by the seven levitical trumpeters, and followed by the military regiments in order.

On the seventh march of the seventh day, at the sound of the sacred trumpets, the people raise a great shout, like the acclamations of the temple liturgy—or the great *Amen* of the Roman church in St Jerome's time—and the walls of Jericho come tumbling down.

Jos 6:17ff

The sacred character of the destruction of Jericho is made clear at the end of the narrative as it had been at the beginning. The theophany leads through the military ritual to the *herem*. The city is set apart as belonging to Yahweh and removed from human use. It is destroyed.

Similar bans are recorded in Near Eastern inscriptions: the famous Moabite stone, for example, declares that Mesha, in 839 or so, put the city of Nebo under a sacred ban because the inhabitants and their property had been 'devoted to Ashtar-Chemosh' (cf also Deut 20 : 16–18 and Lev 27 : 28).

The corporate nature of the Israelite advance is made clear too in the warning that if any individual Israelite take some trinket for himself it will be counted as if the whole army had fallen to carrying off the spoil. So men, women and children (except of course Rahab and her family), animals, and goods (except of course, says the careful historian thinking of what might be useful in a temple like that which he knew, the silver and gold treasures and the bronze and iron pots) are destroyed.

A curse is placed on anyone who attempts to raise again those walls that Yahweh himself had thrown down. The historian is evidently thinking here of Hiel of Bethel who seems at his rebuilding of Jericho to have sacrificed his two sons as a foundation offering, or at least to have suffered the deaths of his sons during the time of the rebuilding (1 Kg 16 : 34). The historian puts in the curse on the sons of the builder because he is certain that it is going to be fulfilled by events which are by the time of writing already well-known history.

It used to be asserted with innocent confidence by those historians who relish such things that the Jericho which fell to Yahweh was City D at the fourth level, destroyed some time between 1385 and 1250. But recent excavations have shewn that the broken walls and burnt artefacts, once taken to establish the exactitude of the Joshua narrative, belonged to a city deserted probably about 1580. Dr Kenyon's excavations have left little to the literalists—not much more indeed than the possibility of a small fort having been erected on the ruins and sand-hills round the spring that has always encouraged men to set up their homes at this site.

The historian was, of course, quite unaware of all this archaeological business. Jericho is presented in his story as a location of meaning. Wherever Yahweh acts nothing, not even a walled city, can stand against his will.

1. Can we now accept that any war should be accounted 'holy'?

2. The historian of the capture of Jericho believed not in the power of armies but in the effectiveness of the liturgy in the world of action. Do we share his belief in this kind of effectiveness?

Jos 7:1 ff. The story of Ai

All has gone well. Yahweh has given them the territory held by the men of Jericho. It is obvious that the Israelites should go on in this divine campaign and that they should be given town after town. This is how the historian would like to set out his narrative.

But there is a stubborn piece of evidence that prevents such a straightforward narrative of success. The attack on Ai which followed that on Jericho, and was part of the same campaign, was not at the first a success. The town had to be fought for with some energy. How was such a reversal to be accounted for? The historian applied here his principle of covenant loyalty. The army must have failed to obey the demands of Yahweh concerning the *herem*. This alone would account for the repulse of Yahweh's army by a pagan force.

The archaeologists are no more helpful about Ai than they are about Jericho. It would seem that Ai was a heap of stones during the life of the historian *and* during the period of the entry into Palestine. The story may well have arisen as an early attempt to account for the ruins at this place. The element of defeat and ban disobedience belongs to an elaborated version of such a tale of the ruins.

Joshua sends out scouts, as he had done before the attack on Jericho. There is at least this military precaution in the divine plan for the conquest. The spies return with the happy intelligence that the city could well be taken without the mustering of the whole Israelite army. The way from the camp at Gilgal to Ai was uphill all the way and so not very attractive to the Israelites who were still supposing that Yahweh was about to take the place for them anyway. Perhaps the fact that Joshua employed fewer troops than were later discovered to have been required was the kernel of an older story which simply stated the military realities of the case. The historian, however, wants to make the meaning of such facts clear to his readers.

The attack having been made and repulsed by the garrison of Ai, some inquiry had to be made as to the causes of such a surprising event. Investigation brought the ugly fact of disobedience into the open. Yahweh had not been with the army, it had not been Yahweh's army, because the *herem* had been broken. It is interesting that the historian has avoided questions about whether the

presence of Yahweh was attached to the ark by not saying whether the ark went on the raid against Ai or not.

Joshua tears his clothes and puts dust upon his head
in the traditional attitude of ritual mourning. Like the
times when they were hungry in the desert there comes
upon the dispirited Israelites a sense that it would have
been better not to attempt the whole business of escape
and victory if such things were to happen. Nothing ever
goes right, was their thought. Joshua does not want to
work with an army which has the reputation of running
away. He becomes himself for a moment a victim of
mumbliness.

But Yahweh is Yahweh. The Lord of Armies puts new
spirit into his chosen leader. He declares again the link
between sin and punishment within the covenant, and
commands a ritual cleansing of the community.

The lottery is governed by Yahweh and is not a re-
lapsing into the hazards of chance. Yahweh does not revenge himself with a blast of fury. He simply points out
the cause of the failures of the attack on Ai and leaves
the defence of his honour to his people. They know what
to do when Achan is discovered. He has brought ruin on
the whole people and the corporate sense of Israel determines that only if the congregation gets rid of the sinner
will Yahweh's grace be poured out on them again.

It may seem odd to us that Achan was told to praise
Yahweh for discovering his offence. The historian did
not notice anything odd here. What he noticed was that
Achan had been misled by the beauty of a robe of Shinar.
This detail is significant. To the historian Shinar was a
name of Babylon. He is suggesting here that those Jews
who in his time were flirting with the customs and
luxuries of life in Babylon were treasuring up disaster
for themselves.

The fancies of archaeologists must be restrained here as elsewhere. Sir Flinders Petrie discovered at Tell el-'Ajjul a heap of human bones, gold ornaments and other objects, with all the signs of having been burnt together. It would be rash to join him in the supposition that something like Achan's punishment had here been meted out.

Jos 8:1 ff. The taking of Ai

Here a number of sources have been combined to give an odd effect of double vision. The ambush is laid in verses 3–9 and then again at 10–13; Joshua spends a night among the people at verse 9 and spends it again at 13 (having got up so early that there was time for work and a nap before breakfast, cf Prince Hal's satiric account of Hotspur's morning).

Yahweh's presence on this occasion is signified by the effect of Joshua's holding of his javelin—his outstretched hand is rather like those of Moses during the battle against the Amalekites (Ex 17:8–12). The hand is kept up until the end of the day and the execution of all the inhabitants of Ai has been effected (8:26). The detail of the king of Ai's body being taken down at sunset indicates that the historian is aware, though Joshua of course would not have been, of the new rule of Deut 21:23. The modernity of the rule, as distinct from its being the codification of an ancient custom, is shewn from the watch of Rizpah over the exposed bones of Saul's family (2 Sam 21:10 ff).

Jos 8:30 ff. The celebration

The sacred character of the campaign that opened with the theophany leads at the end to the erection of an altar

to Yahweh in accordance with the demands of the law.
This is built upon Mount Gerizim (not Mount Ebal) and
it became in the historian's time the central shrine of
the Samaritans (cf Jn 4:20 f). There the people gather
round the ark to hear Joshua read the law.

The historian imagines a scene like that described in
the work of the Chronicler when Ezra read the law to
the people who had at last settled in Jerusalem (Neh 8).
This ceremony brings to an end the first campaign of
the Israelites in Canaan, just as the ceremony in Joshua
24 brings to an end the conquest and settlement of the
whole land.

*1. Does it seem odd that the one history should con-
tain so formal a narrative as that of the Jericho capture,
and so psychologically naturalistic a story as that of the
Israelites' wavering at Ai?*

*2. The concept of the honour of God evidently meant
much to Joshua, and was a motive force in the career of
Thomas à Becket, but is it an effective idea for us? Do
we accept a duty to defend God?*

*3. What causes are there for the present great interest
in archaeology, and are they at work in our reading of
the old testament?*

3

The conquest
Jos 9:1–12:24

Jos 9:1 ff. The second campaign

Jos 9:1. The pagan inhabitants of Canaan conspire to
form a coalition against the stranger Israelites who seem
to win by trumpet blowing, ambuscadoes, and cultic
festivals.

Jos 9:3 ff. Gibeon

The men of Gibeon, however, were known by the historian to be ministers of the temple in Jerusalem. And it
was common knowledge also that before their Jerusalem
ministry the Gibeonites had tended the great sanctuary
of Yahweh in their city. A sanctuary to which Solomon
the great king had gone to receive from Yahweh at the
beginning of his reign the divine gifts of wisdom and
wealth (1 Kg 3:4 ff, 2 Chron 1:3–12). The historian
had to explain somehow the survival of these foreigners
in the midst of Israelite society. He found the needed
explanation in the story of the old wineskin trick.

The story tells itself. A nice piece of rapscallion cunning deceives the Israelites, and they later find the story
enjoyable enough to keep it in their camp tellings. The
primitive peasant fun of the tale has much in common
with the tale of uncle Laban's sheep and the stripped

wands. The reader is meant to see the trick as effective only because Joshua and the elders had not attended to the proper order of things. They did not consult Yahweh before making a treaty with the foreigner. The people have a right to grumble when a whole area of Canaanite land is taken from them and given to these strangers. It must appear to them that what Yahweh had prepared for Israel had been thrown away on a batch of wicked aliens.

The determination to make the Gibeonites into menial servants in the cult is the mechanism by which the historian makes the story account for the presence of these folk in the contemporary temple service. Thus comes the situation 'down to the present day' (Jos 9: 27).

The Gibeonite confederation of Horite towns occupied a strategic position in the centre of the other Canaanite settlements, so the others could not simply allow their position to be weakened by such a breach in their lines of defence.

Jos 10: 1 ff

At this point we come to one of those frequent occasions when the story of the conquest in Joshua is seen to conflict with that told in Judges. In Joshua, generally, the conquest is presented as quite a simple matter, a divinely guided progress of the whole nation from victory to victory, spoilt and delayed at times by the sinful negligence of Yahweh's law by the military men of Israel, but otherwise uninterruptible.

In Judges we are given a picture of the various tribes making piecemeal and not all that effective attacks upon the Canaanite strongholds that Joshua had already taken with perfect ease.

It may be, of course, that the discrepancies are to be
brought together by the supposition that the work of
Joshua and his officers was effective only for their own
time, and that later the Israelites were beaten back from
the positions he had gained. Still later the Israelite tribes
had one by one, perhaps, summoned enough energy to
make individual efforts to recover the old lands that they
had once held. This second time the Canaanites were
ready for them and not so easily dislodged.

But it is probably wise to consider carefully how, for
example, it is that in Jg 1:1–20 territory so totally conquered as that of South Canaan is said to have been by
Joshua in Jos 10, should need to be attacked as if for the
first time, no relic of the previous Israelite military
occupation surviving.

Similar difficulties occur when the narratives of the
occupation of Hebron are examined. Jos 10:36 puts the
conquest of this area to the credit of Joshua, but Jg 1:20
declares that it was not conquered until after Joshua's
death.

Again, even if we remain within the limits of Joshua
itself, similar difficulties arise. For example, Jos 10:38
states that Joshua conquered Debir, but at 15:17 it is
clear that Debir was in fact occupied by Othniel though
during Joshua's lifetime. This has to be thought upon
before the reader turns to consider the statement in
Jg 1:13 that Debir was occupied only after the death of
Joshua. A similar set of difficulties arises about Gaza (cf
Jos 10:41, 13:2 and Jg 1:18).

The most likely solution of this kind of difficulty is to
be found in a happy acceptance of the fact that neither
the author, or authors, or editors, nor their readers
among their contemporaries, were so concerned when
they talked of the material of Joshua or Judges with

historical details of persons, campaigns, towns and dates, as they were with the proclamation of Yahweh's relation to his people. The historian who put Joshua together evidently thought that this relation would be best seen as one of power, and likened the conquest to a liturgical manifestation of wonder. Nothing was less strenuous than the take-over of the land. The historian of Judges thought that this relation would be best seen as one of love, and he likened the conquest to a persevering and hardly won triumph over immense difficulties. The Deuteronomist editors of both books evidently did not find it impossible to appreciate the work and outlook of both original historians. It would be a sad comment upon the understanding we now have of the historian's craft if we could not include works which the Deuteronomist knew to speak of his country's history effectively.

1. When we read such a story as that of the tricksy Gibeonites do we advert to any didactic purpose of the historian? Ought we to look for such a purpose?

2. Does it offend or please that the conquest narrative of Joshua is not always in harmony and sometimes is in conflict with that of Judges?

Jos 10:6–5. The defeat of the kings

Two traditions are brought together in this account, one dealing with the southern Canaanite towns and the other with the five kings. The historian has made a nicely integrated story from his material. The tale rattles along from the first scene of the conspirators' meeting at Jerusalem.

The Israelite army marches in one night from Gilgal, which was evidently still being used as a base-camp as in the first campaign in Canaan, and arrives suddenly upon the kings as they sit round Gibeon. The Israelites chase the royal armies across the country, Yahweh all the while bouncing the great stones of heaven on their heads.

A second account of the fight evidently gave more credit to the Israelite armies than to the hail-stones. The historian has simply added a piece from this poetic account to the first story. The royal armies are chased under the hail-stones—which land always on the heads of the pagans and never on the pursuing Israelites—but Joshua, fearing that when evening comes those retreating will find cover in the shadows and escape him, asks for a staying of the sun so that all may be slaughtered. The snatch of poem comes from the same collection as David's lament for Saul.

Nothing of much value is to be gained from considerations as to just what we are to understand by the sun's ceasing to move, since we are at any rate most of us committed to the other convention which demands that we think the earth stopped. We must leave the physicalities out of consideration and take it either as a wonder which lengthened the hours of daylight, a wonder easily within Yahweh's power, or as a metaphor intended to put across the Israelites' sense that through the goodness of Yahweh they had had a long day's victory.

Jos 10:16 ff

That the story of the five kings is tacked on to the story of the pursuit can be detected in a quick review of the text. Verse 15 is obviously a concluding statement. Verse 19 however suggests that the pursuit is still going on. It comes from a different source and is added here because it seemed a fun tale to the historian. It also quite satisfactorily accounted for the heap of stones at Makkedah, 10:27.

The kings are treated first of all as if they were captives of the Egyptians, who had been seen by the Israelites to place their feet on enemy necks, and then as if they were under the regulations of the Deuteronomic law, being cut down at evening—their treatment is thus a summing up of the movement in Israelite social customs from Egypt to law.

Jos 10:28 ff

This episode seems to belong to a very early account of the campaign; it says nothing of the allies of the king of Jerusalem, nothing of the cave execution, and lists the kings as separate and successive foes. It would appear that some historian has done a conflating work to bring the five kings together. The process of conflation may well be older than the work of our man. Our historian has edited the material so that it should fit the grand notion of the conquest being an easy progress through the land.

The literary form is rather like a series of stepping stones placed strangely enough in a circle. Jericho provides the pattern for the treatment of Libnah, Libnah that for Lachish, Lachish that for Eglon, Eglon that for Hebron, Hebron that for Debir. And when the historian comes to Debir, in order that it may be apparent that nothing has been lost in the process of transferring the treatment from one to another, he says that the last has come round to the first again. Libnah provides the pattern for the treatment of Debir.

1. What is it that makes an intelligent man like Sir

*Isaac Newton consider carefully the astronomical effects
of Joshua's prayer?*

2. *At what point should we pause in our ordinary
scientific and historical investigations of such stories?
How can we discipline ourselves to recognise such a
point?*

Jos 11:1. The Northern kings

Having dealt with the Southern Canaanites Joshua is
ready to tackle the kings of the North. These, like the
southern kings, form an alliance and muster an army 'as
countless as the sands of the sea'. No human power could
oppose such a coalition with any hope of success. The
historian, relying on the promise to carry all before him,
has simply to say that Joshua took the kings unawares
and totally destroyed their armies.

This kind of adventure story reminds me of a popular
radio series when I was a small boy concerned with Dick
Barton, Special Agent. This was written by two authors,
each concocting a week's adventures for the hero. One
of the script-writers decided to see if he could make life
more difficult for the other. He finished his week's
episode with Dick Barton slowly dying from the effects of
a huge blow on the head, chained to the wall of a dungeon
in which the rising water had already reached his chin,
and the whole thing about to blow up at the next second's
strike of an alarm-clock. The script-writer who followed
was not, however, to be trapped by such devices, he knew
his hero and what his audience would credit. The next
episode began with the simple and sublime statement:
'With one bound he was free'. The historian of Joshua
and the conquest is equally assured that Yahweh can
make all things well in an instant.

The northern kings go down and the ban is carried out. The Israelites do not intend to risk another Ai.

Jos 11:15 ff

Like Luke tracing back the line of Jesus until he comes to Adam 'who was the son of God', our historian here traces Joshua's authority back to Moses, who received his order from Yahweh (cf 11:23).

The Judges account of the conquest, which suggests certain difficulties in the subduing of the native Canaanites, receives some support at 11:17–20, but the final verse of chapter 11 gives a sense of winding all to a graceful harmony.

The historian's list in chapter 12 of conquered kings and their territories has the effect in geography that the genealogical lists of the Chronicler have in time—they justify the present by describing the whole of Canaan as from the first entry of the Israelites being held as Yahweh's gift to his people.

4
Settlements
Jos 13:1–22:34

Jos 13:1–19:51. Dividing the spoil

The areas named in the description of the parts of the country not subdued by Joshua belong to groups of Canaanites who were never to belong to the Israelite confederation. The operative words remained: 'in the meantime...'. The apportioning of the land is performed in two stages, the first at Gilgal when Judah and the stronger Joseph tribes received their share, the second at Shechem, after some further fighting, to the lesser tribes. The two accounts derive from different sources and complement each other.

The telling of the story here supposes that the conquered land belonged to all the nation and that it had to be divided among the tribes. The old Trans-jordanian settlements are recognised as official holdings and then the Cisjordanian territories are allotted.

There are three traditions about the management of the sharing-out of the land on the west bank of the Jordan:

(a) 14:1a, 5; 19:49 and 50
   In this tradition the nation itself divided the territory by lot according to Yahweh's instruction to Moses.
(b) 13:7, 14:6, 18:2–10
   Here Joshua is said to have been given the individual

49

task by Yahweh of settling the boundaries of the tribal lands.

(c) 14:1b, 19:51a
Here the presidency of the allotting committee is given to the priest Eleazar, the son of Aaron, and head of the levitical order (cf Num 3:32, 20:25–28).

The settlement of Reuben, Gad and the half-tribe of Manasseh, the stateless character of the wandering levites, and the territory guaranteed to Caleb, having been cleared away, the historian sets out to describe the distribution of land to each of the remaining nine-and-a-half tribes.

This takes him to 19:51, and he is evidently discussing matters of great interest to himself and his first readers. The interest in such matters must have been huge among the early Israelites in order that such lists should be preserved, but it would be rash of me to assume a similar excitement in the minds of the generality of modern readers at the tales of the protest of the Joseph tribe and their being told to clear the hill forests (17:14 ff), the difficulty of determining the northern border of Zebulon's territory (19:27 ff), or the lack of border information for the area of Dan (19:40 ff). Something, however, must be said to account for the Israelites' great business with these things.

At the beginning of the covenant the wonder of Israelite life had been the presence of Yahweh as friend of the people. They were a people because Yahweh had called them together. They could be a people wherever there was a place for a congregational acknowledgement of Yahweh. Once they had occupied Canaan the land became a witness to Yahweh's presence, and to possess a part of the land became for each Israelite tribe and each

individual Israelite a proof of the claim to belong to the
people of Yahweh.

The incident of Naboth's vineyard shows how much
the inherited share an Israelite had in the promised land
meant to later generations. Jezebel could not appreciate
the feelings of the ordinary Israelite farmer, but her
Israelite husband knew what was opposed to his will and
thought the traditional argument unanswerable. That is
why he sulked. The story of Naboth's vineyard has more
horror in it than mere land-grabbing or murder. It is
concerned with a foreigner's attempt to take away an
Israelite's claim to be a member of Yahweh's congregation.

Once the Israelites had realised through their experience of the exile that it was possible for them to be
separated from the land Yahweh had given them, then
of course it became of vital importance to get back to the
land of the founding fathers and secure themselves
against such wanderings again. The whole future of
Yahweh's people and of Yahwism in the world seemed to
the historian, writing after the exile, to be linked with
the task of remaking the life of the people on the land.

Thus the delimitation of what was the land and what
each tribe should properly possess in the land became the
definition of the nation and its members. The boundaries
became in the minds of the returning Israelites the out-
ward signs of Yahweh's graciousness towards the nation,
and of Israel's loving response. The maintaining of those
boundaries became the criterion of Israel's measuring up
to the responsibilities of the covenant.

The long record of the territories of each family group
is thus, for the historian and his contemporaries, a tally
of Israel's claims to belong to the covenant. From these
lists later generations will be able to delimit the applica-

tion of the covenant to those who can prove a family right
to the divinely given estates. The holding of the land is
the criterion of communion.

That the soil itself became holy and that only worship
of Yahweh performed on that holy soil could be reckoned
orthodox and worthy of Yahweh, comes out not only in
the later Jerusalem scribes' limitation of canonicity to
those books which had been written within the frontiers
of Israel, but also in the story of Naaman the general who,
on his conversion to the worship of Yahweh, took away
with him to the gentile court sacks of holy soil on which
to stand in prayer. Worship in spirit and in truth was,
like patriotism, not enough.

Those who find the land-lists tedious are obviously
not to be entertained by modern parallels, but that the
sense of land conferring privilege—and this quite apart
from whether a man owns the land or lives on it or not—
is still at work in English society may be discovered by a
perusal of the court and gossip columns of the newspapers
and their talk of the Duke of Norfolk and his peers.

The division of the land is worked out at Shiloh the
great shrine, once the sacred place of the Canaanites of
the district but now given over to Yahwism. It must have
been an important place in Israelite estimation since
after it had been devastated by the Philistines (1 Sam 4)
it was rebuilt and survived until after the collapse of 587
(cf Jer 41:5) and seems to have been still the scene of
some cultic functions for some time into the exilic period
(cf Jer 7:12 ff). It is curious that the Danites seem at
Jgs 18:31 not to know about Shiloh, and it may be that
there were periods when the shrine was deserted.

Jos 20:1–9. The cities of refuge

The authority of Moses' intention (cf Num 35:9 ff) as

described by the priestly writer is alleged to authenticate the sanctuary towns, and the late date of this section is indicated by the reference to the high priest, for his office did not come into existence until after the exile. We have here, then, a piece of clerical writing which appeals to authority and suggests that a modern institution is part of 'tradition'.

The cities of refuge were intended to enable Israelite quarrels to be brought to an end without recourse to the bloody business of the vendetta. The feud was the most likely response of a family to the injury of one of their members. Few would stop to ask why a man had been attacked by members of another family. So a pursuit would begin across the country. The old tribal customs were doubtless necessary in the past to protect the tribesmen from all kinds of other horrors, but it would be a wretched society if these things were kept going after the settlement of the land.

Like the law of 'an eye for an eye' the cities of refuge were designed to bring the people further along the road to social harmony. They were curbs delimiting the sphere of revenge and introducing a mechanism for legal forgiveness—they afforded a breathing-space for an accused man and his accusers to discover the truth of the matter before a series of revenging killings was begun.

Jos 21:1–43. The levitical cities

The tradition in Israel was that the levites, men who relied upon Yahweh in every sphere of life, Yahweh's servants at all times, were never settled on particular plots of land. They lived in small family groups serving the various tribes and maintaining the shrines all over the land. They were recognised as a tribe only through their sacral function.

To be tribeless would be to lack a claim in Israel, but to be a tribe in the usual sense was impossible for the levites who had duties all over the tribal area. So the levites were allotted scattered towns which provided them with home-bases from which they could go out to serve among the tribes. Originally they seem to have been given four towns in each tribal area.

The priestly author of this section was mainly interested in the Aaronite levites whom he therefore says occupied cities of the south round Jerusalem, the others he regarded as little more than temple slaves and these are placed in the territories of the northern tribes.

Jos 22:1 ff. The dismissal of the Transjordanian tribesmen

In a passage reflecting more a wish than a history the writer describes how the men of the tribes across the Jordan river remained loyally with their fellows in the covenant until they had all gained territory for their settlements. Joshua then dismisses the Transjordanians with thanks and booty. They return happily to the lands which have been quietly waiting for them during the conquest campaigns.

Jos 22:9 ff. The dispute about the altar

The historian wrote at a time when the central shrine of Jerusalem was struggling to achieve once more the status of the one legal sanctuary of Yahweh. He could not well allow the claims of any other shrine to be of ancient foundation and pleasing to Yahweh.

Evidently the old cult of the stone circle shrine was still claiming to be acceptable to Yahweh and the priests of the shrine were demanding to be allowed to continue their services. The historian had to put some stop to this. He tells a story which puts an end to any suggestion that there had been a time when more than one sanctuary had been accepted by the tribes as a proper place for the liturgical worship of Yahweh.

The altar is built on the west bank at the place where the Israelites crossed the Jordan (cf Jos 4:1–9 which reflects this same controversy).

The congregation of Israel, the full complement of religious authority, is summoned to deal with this heretical cult. There is a muster at Shiloh, and Phinehas the priest, with the representatives of the ten tribes of Cisjordan, is sent to rebuke the Transjordanians. His speech, 22:16, is that of a well-known defender of the faith (cf Num 25:6–9, Ps 106:28–31), and quite naturally refers to his experience at Peor, and the sin of Achan, and quite unnaturally (for a man of this period) makes the complacent remark that Cisjordan is really the only true Israel. Phinehas essays the opinion that the Transjordanians may only keep the faith if they leave their lands and come to live with the good tribes across the river.

The whole of Phinehas' speech is based upon the later circumstances of the state. The claims of Jerusalem are given a spurious extension into the past. And the reply of the Transjordanian tribes is based upon the same assumption of a centrally organised cult. The excuse made for the altar is that it was not really an altar at all —no sacrifice was ever intended to be offered in this high place—it was in fact a sign that the Transjordanian tribes wanted to be counted as members of the congregation round the Jerusalem altar. Just as the heap of stones set up by Laban and Jacob (Gen 31:48), is a witness to their perpetual alliance, so the altar on the river bank is

a stone of witness to the perpetual confederation of those
who live on the far side of the river-divide and those who
live in the land itself.

*1. What kinship has the Israelite's feeling for his
farmstead with our ordinary delight in what is ours?*

*2. Can we envisage a religious faith that would not
demand expression in individual or corporate ownership
of land and buildings? Are such things necessary for the
continuance of belief?*

3. What significance has an altar for us?

*4. Does it affect our reading of Joshua that the text
has undergone several tendentious redactions?*

5
Covenant liturgy
Jos 23:1–24:33

Jos 23:1–16. Joshua's farewell

Joshua receives Yahweh's best gift of old age and sum-
mons all Israel, the community of the covenant, as witnesses to Yahweh's loyalty to his people. This scene of
witnessing complements the scene at the stone circle on
the Jordan bank.

The scene at the stone circle is concerned with defin-
ing which men have a part in the covenant. Joshua's
gathering of the elders is concerned with affirming what
Yahweh has done for the members of the covenant. The
connecting word here is 'witness'.

The speech of Joshua moves from consideration of the
land which has been conquered and the land which has
yet to be conquered, to the fundamental truth of the
covenant set down in the law of Moses. The historian
makes his point that at the end of all the swash-buckling
Joshua is not to be summed up in military terms but is to
be understood as a man careful for the due religious
service of Yahweh. Joshua's last message is not that the
people are to take up arms again and conduct a final
campaign against the Canaanites, but that Yahweh will
give them the land. All they have to do is to keep to the
straight way that Yahweh has shewn them and to hold
themselves aloof from the contagion of the foreigner.

57

Above all they are to keep themselves clean of all contact with the gods of the foreigner.

The threat of Yahweh's anger is added to make firm the purpose of any wavering Israelite caught by the winsome smile of a Canaanite girl, or unable to keep himself from joining in the dance of the hill shrines, or speculating on matters of comparative religion.

Jos 24:29. After this rather dull piece of valedictory exhortation in which Joshua has said all the right things there should follow the account of his death and burial, and the significant tribute to his memory that while he and those who had been taught by him led Israel the people remained in the true service of Yahweh. But there have been inserted at this point pieces of material which the editor required for his further purposes.

(i) Jos 24:33. The priestly editor of a post-exilic time who had earlier been responsible for the insertion of that third element in the narratives of the division of the territory among the tribes, the priestly presidency of Eleazar, thought that the climax of the whole account of Israel's history at this early period should be the telling of the death of the son of Aaron and this great priest's burial.

Perhaps he was thinking of Joshua and Eleazar as new Moses and new Aaron. He was certainly wanting to impress his contemporaries with the historic importance of the priest in the very first days of Israel's occupancy of the promised land.

(ii) Jos 24:1–28. Joshua at Shechem

The editor had also a splendid piece of material describing a meeting of the tribes at Shechem as the congregation of Yahweh. This he certainly could not leave out of his account, but he did not know where it went in the chronology of early Israel. Nor do we. It may be that Jos 24 was the first ending of the account and that Jos 23 was intended to substitute for it in a Deuteronomistic revision. It is however at least as likely that while Jos 23 replaced some earlier ending, Jos 24 was not that ending. Was not, indeed, any ending at all, but rather was an incident within the body of the history. Perhaps it was a duplicate narrative of the Shechem covenant meeting described in 8 : 30–35 of our present text. At any rate whether Jos 23 was meant to replace it or no someone had the good sense to copy Jos 24 into the text. Jos 24 provides us with a splendid narrative of a covenant ceremony and one which doubtless contains a deal of primitive material however much that material has been subject to Deuteronomistic or other editing.

At Shechem, under the great oak in the ancient Canaanite shrine (like the tree of Woden that St Boniface cut down, being evidently less able than Joshua to include other people's sacred objects among his own), Joshua leads the people in a service of covenant renewal.

The oak was evidently so much a part of Canaanite notions of the sacred that the word for both goddess and terebinth was *'elat*. Perhaps the Canaanite pantheon had room for more than one minor lady or power like the Greek *Dryas* who took her name from *drys*, the oak in which she dwelt. E. M. Forster's *Road from Colonus* shows how such notions about trees may be continued into christian societies. Jos 19 : 33, where the oak of Zanaannim near Kedesh is used as a famous boundary mark for tribal territories, is evidence enough that the tree of Shechem was not alone in being venerated at this time.

Shechem, like Bethel and Jerusalem, was on the trade
route that came from Mesopotamia through Aleppo and
Damascus to the south. Abraham came along this route
and arrived in Shechem having stopped long enough in
Damascus to adopt one of its citizens as his business
partner (Gen 15: 1–3). All Israel must have been aware
of the stories which linked the pagan tree with their own
holy history. They must have known that it was at this
tree that Abraham had received the promises of Canaan
(Gen 12: 6 ff). And here he had erected an altar (Gen
12: 8 and 18) which was later repaired by Jacob, who had
bought land at Shechem (Gen 33: 20), and who had
buried under the oak the Mesopotamian statuettes and
ear-rings that his people were still clutching (Gen 35: 4).
Perhaps the pilgrimage from Shechem to Bethel com-
memorated this patriarch's journey.

That the sanctity of the oak-tree was generally accepted
by the Israelites despite its Canaanite associations is a
theory sustained by these references from both J and E
sources, by the declaration of Moses (Deut 11: 30) and
the story of Abimelech (Jg 9: 37). And it would appear
that at least until the final editing of Joshua men came to
the shrine to look at the burial place of Joseph.

It is of some interest, therefore, that there is no reference in the Joshua conquest narrative to the storming or
capture of Shechem or to its making a peaceful treaty
with the tribesmen. The site was perhaps so holy in later
times that it was impossible to think of its being sacked
by the soldiery, and yet so Canaanite originally that it
was impossible to suppose that Joshua had not attacked
the town and put it to the ban. There is some evidence
that Shechem was originally the city of Lab'ayu, the lion
man, who fought against both southern and northern
Canaanites, and perhaps he and his descendants wel-

comed the forces of Joshua who were fighting against the same enemies. The city may have been taken into the new society without a fight. On the other hand there is some archaeological evidence that the old sanctuary at Shechem was destroyed during the twelfth century, that is just as Joshua arrived in Canaan. Perhaps the old shrine was completely destroyed by the pillaging Israelites and a wholly new sanctuary erected for the cult of Yahweh on the site. The situation in Jerusalem, where the Israelites took over a Canaanite shrine-city and while allowing the original inhabitants to go on living in the place built a great shrine for Yahweh, shows that it was possible for a town to pass from one religious service to another without too much fuss. At any rate, whatever happened to bring Shechem under the Israelite rule, the historian remains quite quiet.

Jeroboam built his house at Shechem (1 Kg 12:25) for reasons which must have included the gathering to himself of the religious sentiment surrounding the old sanctuary even during the first glorious days of the new Jerusalem cult, and the town must have remained the royal residence of the north until Omri bought Samaria. Little stone altars from the period of the monarchy have been excavated at the site and there is an amount of archaeological evidence of the cult having been continued at Shechem for a very long time. At the last editing of Joshua the holiness of the site was recognised but obviously its northern past had to be ignored, so it was first placed in the list of cities of refuge (Jos 19:7), and then declared to have been one of the levitical towns (21:21).

The covenant renewal

In what must be a typical cultic review of Israel's history

as it was recited at later congregational gatherings, Joshua proclaims the moments of Yahweh's favour. The history is announced by Yahweh himself:

(a) Abraham is brought from Ur to the land of Canaan, 24:3;

(b) The promise is continued through Isaac, Jacob and Esau, 24:4;

(c) The people are then led by Moses and Aaron (the addition of Aaron suggests a priestly revision of this credal statement) out of Egypt, 24:5;

(d) The incident at the Reed Sea is given some elaboration, 24:6–7;

(e) The desert journey ends in the Jordan crossing and the occupation of the promised land, 24:8;

(f) The Baalam incident (cf Num 22–24), which delighted the Israelites; it occurs at Jos 13:22, Deut 23:4, Neh 13:2 and Mic 6:5;

(g) The taking of Jericho is obviously a great moment in the sacred history; it is the sign for Joshua's contemporaries, and for those of the historian, that all Israel's enemies will yield to Yahweh;

(h) And, since an already cultivated land is wholly theirs, Israelites have no pioneering worries, they simply sit in their homes drinking the vintage wine and eating the olives that the Canaanites provide for them.

From the recitation of the history Joshua leads into the proposal that those men of Israel who are now aware of what Yahweh has done for them in the past and of what he promises for the future shall at this moment declare their willingness to serve him.

Joshua offers his fellows a rhetorical choice. They may choose between Yahweh and all foreign gods from Mesopotamia and Canaan. The ritual acknowledgment of

Yahweh, which goes again through the history and ends
with the cry 'We will serve Yahweh', is probably taken
from the affirmations of the cult in Jerusalem. After the
first acknowledgement comes the second versicle: Joshua
again demands that the Israelites obey Yahweh, and the
second response: 'It is Yahweh we wish to serve'. The
declaration of witness is like that of the elders at 23: 3,
and is followed by a third exhortatory versicle, and a
third affirmation: 'It is Yahweh our God we choose to
serve'. The triple demand and response here may be
helpful for our appreciation of what is going on in the
appendix (our chapter 21) to John's gospel where Peter
three times affirms his love for Jesus. The charge 'Feed
my sheep' seems to occupy a place very like the three-
times charge to the people. Both are renewals, it might
be noted, of earlier accepted constitutions of the community. It might also be useful to consider whether the
new testament's talk of Peter as 'stone', deriving of course
from Jesus' happy pun, is not given further significance
by the taking into account of the setting up of the stone of
witness, 24: 27 (cf Jos 4: 7, 22: 26 and Gen 28: 10–22).
Peter, like the people of the Shechem meeting, is three
times charged to maintain the divinely established life
of the community and to be an unshakeable witness to
the faith. 'Witness' seems at least as useful a notion as
'foundation' in this context.

It used to be generally asserted with some confidence,
and still is suggested by some commentators, that we are
dealing here with a covenant form that derives from
Near Eastern and particularly Hittite suzerainty treaties.
This is, I think, to go beyond the bounds of the text in an
imaginative way. There is no suggestion in Jos 24 that a
covenant is being arranged. Rather the people are con-
firming with an oath their adherence to a covenant

already operative in their community. They are giving their word. The Hebrew terms for the covenant, notably *berit*, derives from the ritual slaughter of animals (cf Gen 15:9–8), and not from oath-taking ceremonies. But the kind of renewal described in Jos 24 is certainly related to Sumerian and Hatti alliance-ceremonies which are properly oath-takings and termed so (cf my discussion of these matters in the section on 'the gentile neighbours' in the *New Catholic Commentary on Holy Scripture*). Such a ceremony, which certainly might be performed by those already allied (cf the renewal of the agreement between the Davidic line and Hiram of Tyre, 1 Kg 5:1–12), would have moved, like the Jos 24 narrative through (i) a naming of the suzerain, (ii) an account of the historical events leading to the present agreement, (iii) the clauses of the agreement, (iv) arrangements for the witnesses of the text, and (v) curses on any signatory who breaks the alliance. We have in this section of the book not a pattern of a covenant-making ceremony but a covenant-renewal ceremony, probably patterned on contemporary political agreements. That Joshua himself shaped the renewal ceremony on such models is of course more doubtful than that the historian so devised his account of the Joshua ceremony that its treaty-renewal character and its liturgical character were both quite recognisable.

The service of Yahweh

The meaning of service in this context needs to be looked at carefully. The service to which Joshua and his people bound themselves is to be understood in relation to that service the Israelites had done Pharaoh in Egypt. At the moment of the exodus Yahweh says to Pharaoh: 'Let my son go that he may serve me' (Ex 4:23, cf also Ex 7:16,

8:16, 9:1, 9:13 and 10:3). The Hebrews exchange one slave-owner for another.

And Yahweh makes his status as slave-owner quite clear by his consistent proclamation to the people that he has brought them out of Egypt. 'To bring out' means to redeem, to buy back in the market-place. The Hebrews are slaves that Yahweh has, either by asserting of right or by bargaining to have his own again, made into members of his slave-household.

The passover eve ceremony, even now, contains a section beginning: 'Once our fathers were slaves in an alien slavery but now God has drawn us into his slavery'. The meaning of the slavery stated here is that intended by St Paul in his letter to the Romans: 'You have been freed from slavery to sin to become slaves to righteousness' (Rom 6:18) and from this concept of 'service' as a slavery to Yahweh, which was expressed in the life style of the covenant demands and in the worship of Yahweh at the tent, the shrine and the temple, came a realisation that to be the slave of Yahweh was to be a free man. Service to the truth emancipates a man.

So the liturgy became a celebration at once of Yahweh's lordship and Israel's freedom. The new testament concept of redemption as a freeing into truth, a freeing manifested in work for others and participation in the liturgical meal of the community, certainly has its origins in the Israelite understanding of Yahweh's redemption of Israel.

1. What can it matter to a christian reader that Yahweh gave a land to the men of Israel? Do we look for a similar grant of territory in which to keep our faith among the wicked modern nations?
2. Where do we draw the line between our sensible

civilised acceptance of other men's manners and beliefs and the indifference of the infidel which is so forcefully condemned in Joshua?

3. What difficulties occur to us when it is proposed that only in the service of God is man truly free?

A liturgical conclusion

The considerations to which a study of the last sections of the book of Joshua leads prepare the reader, perhaps, for a further notion.

A reading of the Joshua account of the entry of the Hebrew people upon the promised land, may, though certainly I do not think it is likely, suggest that the historian was primarily interested in making a proper chronological record of the events 'just as they happened'. Events, it is surely manifest, were for this writer disclosures of Yahweh's will and power in the world. The writing of history was understood by this historian as a task within the holy community given him by Yahweh, a task to make clear to the community how Yahweh acts. This being clear to them they will assuredly respond by a celebration of the covenant service of Yahweh. History leads to liturgy.

It seems quite possible that the whole shape of the book is determined by the liturgical cycle of the three Israelite feasts, Passover, Weeks, and Tabernacles. The narrative seems to follow a pattern of three distinct sections each culminating in the celebration of a covenant feast:

(i) the pilgrimage to a shrine and the celebration of Passover, 1 : 1–5, 13;

(ii) the conquest of Canaan and the celebration of a feast concerned, as Weeks was later, with the responsibilities of Israel before the law, 6 : 1–8 : 35;

(iii) the settlement of the land and the Shechem celebration of a feast at which the gathered people
acknowledge Yahweh as the giver of the land and
all its crops, (24:13), a theme particularly appropriate to the agricultural feast of tabernacles. (cf
also the dismissal of the people, Jos 24:28 and the
final verse of the account of Solomon's celebration
of Tabernacles, 1 Kg 8:65)

Just as the description of the allotment of the various
areas of land to the tribes of the confederation constitutes a sacred geography of the holy land, so the description of the distribution of events through the conquest
narrative constitutes a sacred chronology of holy history.
Just as the establishment of the shrine makes plain the
divine donation of the land, so the celebration of the
liturgical year makes plain the divine shaping of the
history.

In Joshua the complementary character of event and
ritual has only tentative expression. A more confident
proposal of such a complementarity is made in the historical writing of the Chronicler.

1 and 2 Chronicles

1

The setting for the temple and its liturgy
1 Chron 1:1–16:43

1 Chron 1:1–8:32. All Israel

The genealogies present a claim to the land. 'We have always possessed this place, the estate has been in our family for generations, it is properly our land now'. Legitimacy is conferred by the past. The past puts the present in a set of formal relations which are recognisable and determinative. The present tribes are tribes because of their formal establishment in the past. Their vocation now is that of inheritors. The tribes of the Chronicler's time had no more wish to be thought self-made men than had Charles II when at the 1660 restoration he dated his reign from the execution of his father in 1649, or have those distinguished Americans who are able to declare themselves II, III or even IV to bear their name.

The importance of the genealogical lists may be gauged by the reference in Jer 22:28–30 to Jehoiachin's genealogical records. Jeremiah tells the record-keepers: 'list this man as childless' because 'none of his descendants will sit on the throne of David'. Jeremiah knows well enough that Jehoiachin had sons (cf 1 Chron 3:17) but if they are not in the official list they have no claim to the royal honours and cannot succeed to the throne. Jeremiah is saying that their not being listed will make it plain to the world that Jehoiachin's sons do not count as members of the line. The list and not the blood is the essential pedigree.

But the Chronicler is not anxious to bind the present by the past. In the first chapters, precisely when he is recounting the past as legitimisation of the present, he keeps the present and its interests to the fore. Thus 1 : 43–54 (cf Gen 36 : 31–43a) magnifies the importance of Edom in the history because it was a state that presented a threat to the Chronicler and his contemporary reader; 2 : 3–7 links Canaanite marriages with national disgrace in order to reinforce a present condemnation of Israelites marrying into those polluted families who had remained in the land during the exile; 4 : 9–10 upturns traditional thought by maintaining that the effect of a name given in the past may be averted by present prayer; and 6 : 16–30 accepts Samuel as a levite even though he did not belong to a levitical family. The tradition of Israel is always employed by the Chronicler with present needs in mind. This is certainly the case of the genealogies in their details and their general function in the book.

1 Chron 8:32–12:40. The king

The genealogy takes the reader up to the family of Saul, 8 : 33–9 : 1, and then the whole lineage is placed in apposition to an account of the citizens of the post-exilic settlement in Jerusalem. The genealogies are designed to place the present in the control of the returning settlers. Those who remained in Palestine, and even those who stayed in the city of Jerusalem, during the conquest, may have been improperly associating with the foreigner and so are to be dispossessed of the past that they may not have a legal claim to consideration in the present.

The main claim is for liturgical jurisdiction at the setting up of the forms of worship that were to obtain in the future Jerusalem. Hence, after a preliminary reference to the tribes of Judah and Benjamin, representing the south, and Ephraim and Manasseh, representing the north, and together standing for 'all Israel', the chronicler goes through the liturgical persons, priests (9:10 ff), levites (9:14 ff), gate-keepers (9:17 ff) and musicians (9:33 ff). Once this cultic matter has been settled the history can be continued. So 8:33 ff is repeated to bring the reader back to the previous material, at 9:35 ff.

The account of the last moments of Saul in chapter 10 is the first description of an historical event. The Chronicler takes the death of Saul to be the first moment in the history of the temple. Working backwards the Chronicler noted that Solomon built the temple according to the plan of David, and that David was entitled to make the order because he had become king after Saul. The legitimacy of the temple depended on the legitimacy of Solomon's kingship, which in turn depended on the legitimacy of David, which was only demonstrable at the death of Saul.

The Chronicler attempted to answer questions about how it was that David, and not one of Saul's sons, was made king by Yahweh. Certainly there were sons of Saul to inherit. The genealogy had just made that clear, though the deaths of four of them at Gilboa (10:2 and 6a) must have suggested a greatly weakened family, and at 10:6b the facts are actually distorted to enhance this suggestion's effectiveness. Certainly also the family was Yahwist, though the *baal* element in the name Meribbaal implies that Jonathan was not wholly devoted to Yahweh's cause. The reason for the passing by of Saul's family was evidently that disloyalty to Yahweh recorded

in Saul's history. He was unfaithful to the word of Yahweh (10:13) and consulted the witch rather than Yahweh
(10:14). The Chronicler is here perhaps referring to 1
Sam 13 and 15 which show Saul as liturgically inade-
quate, and 1 Sam 28 which shows him going from the
liturgy of Yahweh to indulge in necromancy, but the
Chronicler has certainly decided to ignore 1 Sam 28:6
where it is said that Saul consulted Yahweh but got no
response.

This is the first of a series of notable adaptations made
by the Chronicler when he was going over the Deuter-
onomists' account of the period. The second is his choos-
ing that one of the two possible accounts of Saul's death
(cf 1 Sam 31 and 2 Sam 1) which speaks of Saul committing suicide at Gilboa. It may be that the Chronicler
chose the suicidal narrative in order to attach some
smear of blame to the rejected king at his last moment.
Though suicide on the battle-field was not reprehensible
in anywhere near the same way that suicide in other circumstances was, yet something of a like impropriety may
have been attached to this action in the face of defeat. It
is certainly not clear that the Chronicler regarded Saul's
expectation of the Philistines amusing themselves with
his mutilation or sexual abuse as quite reason enough to
justify taking his own life.

A third reorganisation of deuteronomistic material
occurs at 10:6b where the Chronicler has chosen to
ignore the survival of Ishbaal as ruler in the Transjordan
north (cf 2 Sam 2–4) and has suggested that at Gilboa
'all his house' were killed. The Chronicler was only interested in Saul so far as was necessary to account for the
Davidic kingship. Ishbaal represented an irrelevant and
distracting side-issue and therefore ought to be omitted
from the history.

The accusation against Saul of his not consulting Yahweh, the description of his death, and the omission of any reference to his surviving family, all help to clear the way for the reader to see in David a clean start for the kingdom and to put aside any question about what happened to the former royal family.

The arrival of David is made the more impressive by the Chronicler suggesting that at the death of Saul confusion came upon the Israelites who abandoned their cities and ran to the hill caves, and by his description of the triumph of Dagon. In fact the Philistine victory at Mount Gilboa was their last desperate stand against the Israelite forces. They were already beaten when they had this final fling against Saul. The Chronicler, however, has not had an opportunity to tell the Goliath story or the Robin Hood adventures of David's time in the hills, and he had to have something here to present David as the hero of Yahweh.

The story of David's coming to the kingly rule is foreshortened so that nothing open is said of any period during which David ruled Judah at Hebron, and Ishbaal ruled in the north, though the Chronicler has perhaps unwittingly let slip a hint of this period in 11:3 when the elders 'come to the king at Hebron' which is a phrase taken from an account which recorded David's Hebron period. The Chronicler's emphasis is on 'all Israel' coming together for the anointing of David as king of the whole covenant folk. The promise of Yahweh is carried forward.

Given the king who planned the temple, the story now demands that Israel be possessors of the city of the temple. The Chronicler proceeds to an account of the occupation of Jerusalem. This was a simple business, achieved in much the same style as the Joshua conquest of the land.

The account of the capture of the city leads into a description of David's court. That nothing should spoil the picture of a great people and an ideal court moving around the promised king, the Chronicler has suppressed all references in the earlier historians' work to Joab as a man under a curse (cf 2 Kg 2:5) or as ever having angered David. And this Arthurian concept of the court is further developed in the roll-call of the knights, 11:10–47, who fetch the king water from the dangerous well (11:17 ff), who kill a lion on a snowy day (11:22) and conquer an Egyptian giant (11:23). To the great king's court came many other knights who wanted a share in his fellowship (12:1–41) and together they beat back the wicked barbarian (12:22) before sitting down to a splendid feast (12:40).

The huge numbers which appear at every count in our translations probably are not the Chronicler's way of stressing the importance of an event, but derive from our not knowing the significance of some technical terms for units of the Israelite army. They are at any rate not more challenging to our credulity and not less romantically effective than the description of Canaan as a land infested with marauding giants (cf 1 Chron 20:4 ff, with 1 Sam 17, 2 Sam 21:19 which perhaps depend from Gen 15:20, Num 13:33, Deut 2:11 and 3:11, Jos 17:15 and 18:16). Even if we assume that the numbers are correctly translated, it shows little sense of how stories are told to grouse about tallies of such huge numbers and perverse after such grousing to take delight in tales of such huge men.

1. A society that invests the family tree with authority is unlikely to need old folks' homes or to be familiar

with the self-made man. What estimate is to be given of
the profit and the loss in such a society?

2. Would a society be the better for abandoning such
tales as those of Gilgamesh, David and Arthur and
settling for the rough realities of the present?

1 Chron 13:1–16:43. The ark

Given king and court, the Chronicler, like those who
gave a divine dimension to Arthur's story by introducing
the quest of the grail, brings the sacred symbol of the
Israelite community into its history. The king wants the
ark at his court in order to bring a special blessing upon
his enterprise and to demonstrate his own special place
in the divine plan. The Chronicler sees the king's individual desire as the means of bringing the ark into the
centre of the community and to prepare the way for a
sacred society centred upon Jerusalem.

In Samuel the removal of the ark was a semi-military
operation. Here it is a wholly religious procession of 'all
Israel'. Especially to be noted is the consultation of every
chief as to the propriety of the translation of the ark and
the insistence that 'our brothers' in all the regions of
Israel take a part. The appeal to the brothers represents
the desire of the Chronicler to make Jerusalem a religious city for all Israel, including those in his own time
who held to the worship of Yahweh in the territory of
the old northern kingdom, and to maintain the importance of the levites alongside the other priestly assistants.

The story of Uzza seems to us somewhat shocking. The
ark appears to have behaved like some radioactive stock-
pile and flashed out against a man not wearing the
proper protective garments. And this concept of the ark
and Uzza's fate is not far from the Chronicler's own. For

him it was important that Uzza lacked the levitical auth-
orisation, was not a legitimate handler of the sacred, was
not dressed in the appropriate liturgical vestment. Uzza,
in this history, dies because he has violated the rubrics.
And the Chronicler was anxious that every Israelite of
his own day should understand just how important the
rubrics were. Through obedience to the formal requirements of the liturgy, and only through such obedience,
could men come into contact with the divine.

In a sense the troubles modern readers have with the
genealogies and those they have with the death of Uzza
derive from the same source. The Chronicler was anxious
to strengthen the untried and immature society set up
in Jerusalem after the exile. He wanted to encourage
anything which would provide a firm framework for
community life. The genealogies represent a formal past,
a past with a shape, they told men who they were, pre-
vented the onset of an individual identity crisis by giving
names and functions to men. The death of Uzza represents a formal liturgy, a worship with a shape, it tells
men how to act, prevents the onset of a social identity
crisis by giving terms and functions for corporate action.

For us it may seem strange that men should hope for
a new life and a new grace from the public records office
and the ritual. For the Chronicler, society was so pre-
cariously poised at the edge of chaos that the only safety
lay in a strict observance of rule. Genealogy and rubric
represented the modes of survival for the covenant
people.

The ark brings the past into the present. There is in
the story of Uzza and the ark an echo, and most probably
a deliberate echo, of a famous event in the early history
of the covenant. For the appreciation of the structure
and meaning of the whole history of the ark procession

and Uzza's punishment it is instructive to look at the story of the fall of Jericho with its emphasis upon the processional carrying of the ark amid the blaring of the sacred trumpets, and its sequel in the story of Achan who defied the ban (Jos 6 and 7). After the first failure to move the ark David needs to be reassured that Yahweh had not forsaken him. He does not want to get caught up in a series of events that would lead to an echo of the defeat at Ai.

The defeat of the Philistines in the valley of the giants and the burning of the gods tells David that he is not to blame for the failure of the first effort to bring the ark into Jerusalem, and he determines to make another attempt.

In setting out a second time on this business he made sure that the people would abandon their fear through an understanding of what had gone wrong the first time. As to a cultic event of the Chronicler's time, or at least, as to an ideal cultic event that the Chronicler wishfully imagined, 'all Israel' arrives for the translation of the ark in true liturgical style from the house of Obed-edom.

The account of the translation is studded with rubricional terms: *assemble*, 15:3, *sanctify*, 15:12 (cf Ex 19:10–15, 30:19, Lev 10:9), *Alamoth-Sheminith* (cf introductions to Pss 6 & 46), *invoke*, 16:4, *thank* (which means 'to utter the doxology') 16:4. It is replete, too, with liturgical fragments, notice particularly the quotations from Pss 96, 105, 106, 47, 48 and 136 in 16:7–36 and 16:41, and with references to cultic functions of priests, levites, gate-keepers (cf Pss 24:7–10, 118:19–20 and Is 26:2), singers, and trumpet-players (cf Num 10:1–10).

The whole account is designed to impress upon the reader the importance of cultic rectitude. 15:4–10 and

15 : 16–24 are obvious additions to the older 2 Sam 6 account, and are particularly concerned with levites and choristers (cf the regulations about the tending of the ark in Deut 10 : 8, Ex 25 : 13–14 and 38 : 4–5). The levites are told to go through the ritual purification in order to take their part in the liturgy which was allotted them in the services the Chronicler knew. And they are described as fulfilling the law of Moses as they carry the ark to Jerusalem. The past is with this group of levites and they are themselves employed as a useful connection with a past incident. The Davidic pedigree of that group of the levites who sang in the liturgy the Chronicler knew is substantiated by reference to the singers of Chenaniah in the procession to Jerusalem.

Uzza was not properly accoutred when he led the ark from the house of Abinadab. The Chronicler thinks it would be equally horrific if the king put on a vestment that was not properly his. He has therefore to edit the Samuel account of the procession. 2 Sam 6 : 17 has it that David wore the ephod, which was in the Chronicler's time the vestment of the high priest. Therefore, at 15 : 27a, it is made clear that David only wore a levitical mantle. So great a care and so little final result: the Chronicler's caution seems not to have been shared by the man who later edited his account of the procession. Having read 2 Sam 6 : 14 and spotted the discrepancy, the later editor inserted 15 : 27b and thus confused everything.

The Chronicler plays down the part Michal had in 2 Sam 6, because he had no wish to deflect attention from the great king, or to involve him in any scandal. His Arthur was not to be smeared by any misdemeanour of his Guinevere, nor by any improper behaviour of his own. All the Chronicler requires of Michal is that she

reinforce the impression of 10:13 f that Saul's family
was unconcerned with the proper liturgy of Yahweh.

1 Chron 16:4–43. The technical terms of a later age,
to extol, to give thanks, to praise, are said here to belong
to that critical moment when the levites ceased to be car-
riers of the ark, because the ark had ceased its journey-
ing, and therefore might have found themselves redun-
dant. The Chronicler shifts the levites out of the pilgrimage liturgy of the exodus into the stable liturgy of
the temple. He provides them with a history so that they
can defend themselves from those who suggest that they
are intruders in the cultic events of the Jerusalem shrine
and have no authority in Israel.

The Chronicler says that it is at this moment, under
the charge of the great king, that the levites are equipped
with harps, and zithers, cymbals and trumpets. And the
cultic praise of psalmody is set down, with some examples, as showing that from this moment it had been a
levitical duty to lead the people in this congregational
rite.

The apposition of present cultic interests and historical concerns appears at 16:37–8 when the Chronicler
admits that at this time there were two shrines of Yahweh
—and that the great Zadok served at Gibeon. This is a
dangerous set of facts. Jerusalem must be shewn to be
the true and only true shrine of Yahweh in Israel. Otherwise all sorts of places, like Bethel and Dan perhaps,
would start up again. The balance is restored in Jerusalem's favour in the next section of the narrative, but
it is interesting that the Chronicler did not attempt to
suppress the existence of the Gibeon shrine, though he
must have disliked this rival to Jerusalem being shewn

as acknowledged by David, and have suspected the true Yahwism of the old Canaanite city and its 'high place'.

It would seem that the later ascendency of the priests deriving from Zadok, who was originally connected with Gibeon, over the Aaronites (who are here represented by Abiathar), demanded that the only begetter of this levitical line be presented as wholly acceptable to the king and his folk.

1. What attitudes towards God are revealed by our shock at the punishment of Uzza?

2. Would even the most liturgically-conscious of us want so carefully cultic a life as the Chronicler proposes?

3. How great a diversity of liturgical celebration can a community support with equanimity?

2

The temple—preparations
1 Chron 17:1–22:19

1 Chron 17:1–27. The temple

Once the ark was settled in Jerusalem the obvious thing
was to erect a permanent shrine. The Chronicler thinks
it so obvious that he edits out the 2 Sam 7:1 reference to
intervening battles in order to show David thinking of
building the temple immediately on the arrival of the
ark.

At the same time, in contrast with what seems obvious
to men there is the word of Yahweh. David, the king
chosen by divine will, and Nathan, Yahweh's own
prophet, both make a mistake here. They have to be reminded that the heroic period of love between Yahweh
and his Israelites was not one of life in settled homes but
one of packing and unpacking tents, not one of bricks
and mortar but one of personal relations. The house of
bricks that men have designed is discarded for a house of
heirs given by Yahweh.

Yahweh, it is important to observe, refers to these heirs
as ruling over a house and a kingdom which does not
belong to them—the kings are seen as viceroys set upon
the throne to manage things for the Lord. The Chronicler here and at 1 Chron 28:5, 29:23, 2 Chron 6:5,
9:5 f, 13:8, is accepting the view expressed in the enthronement song preserved in Is 9:6:

> For there is a child born for us,
> a son given to us
> and dominion is laid on his shoulders.

The king is given to the people to carry out the will of Yahweh for the community. He has no power for his own whims. This concept was developed into the messianic idea of the servant of Yahweh (cf Is 42:1, 49:3) and shaped the structure of the Mt 3:17, Mk 1:11, and Lk 3:22 narratives of the baptism of Jesus.

Probably the enthronement song in Isaiah is an adaptation of chants sung at Osiris' recognition of the Egyptian pharaoh when the divine rule was asserted again; if so his song and the royal psalms 2, 89 and 132 have given the chants an Hebraic wrench. The concept of the king as viceroy, wholly alien to Egyptian thought of the divine king, is developed by the Chronicler from its rudiments in these songs in a manner quite different from that of the Deuteronomist. Notice, for example, the differences that the Chronicler has made in the presentation of the Nathan prophecy. The Deuteronomist's account in 2 Sam 7:16 is done wholly within dynastic categories and does not develop any directly theological ideas from the Davidic succession.

The Chronicler has, by his theologising of the Jerusalem throne, been able to maintain a continuity of Israelite history under Yahweh, a continuity which was not available to the Deuteronomist. For the Chronicler the king is simply the present mediator of Yahweh's government of Yahweh's people. David, in a different form certainly, is exercising the same authority as Moses, Joshua and the judges. David's authority may, therefore, be properly regarded as one in a sequence of vice-regalities. The Chronicler is ready to accept the idea that the Davidic rule may be followed by other actualisations of

Yahweh's sovereignty. Thus Cyrus reigns by the Lord's power (2 Chron 36:23, Ez 1:2), and Nehemiah and Ezra, and then the Hasmoneans who were descended from Levi, offer further examples of the different ways in which the one rule of Yahweh is exercised over his people.

The Chronicler, therefore, was not much interested in a messianism which invested a person with the primacy among the people. He was much more concerned with the development of a popular messianism, with the development of a holy people, 'all Israel', round the altar of Yahweh. His messianism is communal.

The social activity of the messianic community is brought into focus at the liturgy before Yahweh. The Chronicler's interest is not, as some commentators have supposed, in the vulgar concept of monarchy as he knew it in other nations, but in the grander notion of the service of Yahweh in his temple.

The response of the king to Nathan's prophecy is to go into the tent-shrine of the ark and to pray that his heirs' prosperity be joined irrevocably with that of the people (17:21–25). The reference here to Yahweh's redeeming work in Egypt provides the reader with the necessary hint towards the understanding of what is going on in this section (17:21). From this primal act of rescue at the exodus the history of the tribes as a nation and as men with a king is developed.

1. How is the concept of 'the kingdom of God' to be made viable in our conversation?

2. Does the divine have to have a particular human representative in order to be effective in the world?

1 Chron 18:1–20:8. The holy war and the financing of the temple

The concept of 'all Israel' going out under the leadership of Yahweh to scatter the enemies of Yahweh was elaborated in Joshua. There the conquest of Canaan was said to have been a quite easy matter. The army of Israel was presented as the processional party of Yahweh, and the enemy could offer no resistance to the pilgrimage march. This concept is not maintained in Judges or Samuel, though, of course, the later editors of all this material have inevitably concealed the differences of tone on numerous occasions. There was the more militarist development, for example, of the concept of the holy war as a matter of battles rather than processions, in which Israel's cause was the defence of the honour of Yahweh, in which the army was supported throughout by Yahweh's power, in which defeat could only come to the army of Israel when sin was committed in the camp, and in which the booty at the end of the battle belonged to Yahweh. The idea of the war became more secular still.

The first battles of Saul were fought under this desert code in quite the manner of Joshua's conquest of the Canaanites. The shirking by Saul of his holy war duty after the defeat of Agag and the Amalekites (1 Sam 15) was not an act of graciousness and mercy appropriate to one who had enjoyed the grace and mercy of Yahweh. It was the first act of a series which removed Saul from his place as leader of the armies of Yahweh, for it was an assertion that a man who worshipped false gods was not the king's enemy to the death, and that the wealth of such a man was not so tainted that the king of Israel could not bring himself to touch it. The old theology of the conquest was being supplanted by a royal notion of power. Because Saul took the king's life and goods to be his own he was rejected by Yahweh.

The Chronicler suggests that when Yahweh placed David on the throne there began a new period of holy war. The victories of 18:1–17, 19:1–19, and 20:1–8 are described in such a way that David appears to have been given one easy triumph after another by the power of Yahweh that was with him as it had been with Joshua (cf 18:13). And after these victories the booty was acknowledged to belong to Yahweh and put in the Jerusalem shrine of the ark. The conquest sense of Israel under Yahweh was being re-established by the great king.

The development at this time was in the treatment of the booty taken in the holy war. The wars of David were won by Yahweh and since Yahweh now had a city where he lived among the people, and since the ark had been settled in a shrine, it was possible for the booty to be truly acknowledged as belonging to Yahweh without the destruction of so much wealth and beauty. The wars now provided a booty which could be used by Yahweh in the construction of his temple.

1. What translation can we make of the 'holy war' in order to make it understandable in our present condition? Are we here confronted with an old testament fact that we cannot employ with advantage in our efforts to live up to the christian vocation?

2. Do we find it easy to make the Chronicler's assumption that giving things to the clergy is giving them to God?

1 Chron 21:1–22:1. Obtaining the temple site

The Chronicler does not put much emphasis on the dull political business of the census. 2 Samuel makes it clear here as at the beginning of that book's Davidic narrative that the kingdoms of Israel and Judah, like the rest of the empire, were bound together by their allegiance to the king, by, that is, a personal link. The Chronicler is not much interested in the separate figures in the census returns which point up this independence of the various territories. He is much more interested in the linking of Israel and Judah through their common worship of Yahweh. They form together the liturgical community of 'all Israel'.

The Chronicler elaborates the Samuel account so that David is seen as totally responsible for the plague and fully worthy of the punishment. He does not make it clear what reasons David had for taking the census. He is not concerned with such things as David's political problems. But it would seem that David wanted a tighter administrative control on all parts of the empire because the troubles associated with the rebellions of Absalom and Sheba had brought home to him the uncertainty of his own position. A census would enable him to start a file on each local headsman.

That the court officials were against the taking of the census need not be an indication of their appreciation of the will of Yahweh. They may have been simply rather lazy and have sensed how difficult it was going to be to get the country farmers to cooperate with the census officials. They may, too, have been more aware than David of the grumblings of the people about the central administration and not have wanted to provoke further opposition.

The whole story of the census seems designed to militate against any notion of the king having full and ordinary monarchical power over the people. Yahweh's people are not to be counted as the serfs of any human ruler.

Together with this moral the story bears the practical narrative task of explaining how the temple site came to be acquired by the Davidic house. The plague brought about by the blasphemous census ceases when Yahweh takes further thought for the safety of his people in Jerusalem. The citizens who gathered round his shrine are not to be destroyed. Not this time. The old idea of one man's sin bringing disaster upon the whole people is complemented by the old idea that the punishment of the sinner will remove the danger to the people. The story of David bringing down punishment upon the community is like that of Achan bringing defeat upon the army at Ai, and the remedy is like that of the Joshua situation. The sinner is to be punished.

The Chronicler has found in the story of the plague— and the plague probably began with the census-takers carrying some disease from village to village as they went about their numeration of the country people—both a suggestion of the monarchy being taught its place as viceregency of Yahweh, and a necessary motive power for his temple narrative.

The account of David buying the threshing floor is evidently based on the Gen 23 story of Abraham buying the cave in the field of Machpelah from Ephron the Hittite. The scene is of a great Israelite hero wanting the land of a foreigner, of the foreigner in the oriental manner at first offering the land as a gift, and then being offered and accepting a fair price by the Israelite.

The Chronicler must have had his reason for making the alteration from the Samuel price of fifty shekels of silver. In the narrative as he set it down David pays Ornan six hundred shekels of gold. Perhaps the Chronicler thought it inappropriate that Abraham's burial ground, which cost four hundred shekels of silver, should be valued at a greater price than the site for the great temple of Yahweh. Perhaps also the Chronicler wanted to suggest that each of the tribes paid something towards the price of their common sanctuary and so gave each of them the honour of paying the Samuel price of fifty shekels.

Given the money from the holy war, and the site pointed out by Yahweh as the place where he remembered his love for the people of Jerusalem and forgave their sin, the Chronicler pauses for a liturgical celebration. It is a great thing to have reached this stage of the grand design. The acceptance of the sacrifice was signified by the fire from heaven (cf Jg 6:21, 1 Kg 18:38).

The fire was, however, even more important than a sign that Yahweh had accepted this particular sacrifice for the plague-stricken folk. The fire confirmed Yahweh's acceptance of the site as the place where the burnt offering should be made to him at all times. The site bought by man had now been blessed by Yahweh.

The Chronicler has found a way of accounting for the removal of the sacrifice from Gibeon and the presence of the Zadokite priests in the Jerusalem liturgy. David and the elders in their sack-cloth had been on their way to the Gibeon shrine to ask for Yahweh's mercy on the people. They were stopped at the start of their journey by the angel of Yahweh who made it clear to them that Yahweh's presence was now manifest in their city of Jerusalem. They did not have to go to Gibeon to ask for his mercy. The sacrifice being consumed is the designation of the temple as the place where Yahweh will meet his people in the liturgy. Then David said: 'Here is the House of Yahweh' (1 Chron 22:1).

The Chronicler now dismisses Gibeon. He omits, for instance, the powerful old story of the famine (2 Sam 21) which was caused by the slaughter of the Gibeonites and was brought to an end by the impaling of seven men of Saul's family at the shrine. He would not, of course, have been at all anxious to suggest to his readers that such primitive fertility rites were patronised by the king of Jerusalem. Nor would he have wanted his readers to become interested once more in Saul and his family. And certainly he did not want them to become sympathetically interested.

It must be noted, however, that Solomon's accession incubation at Gibeon was set down in the Chronicler's narrative without any discernible hesitation (2 Chron 1:3–6).

1. What kind of connection, if any, do we see between sin and the catastrophes that come down on some men in this life?

2. Do we find it easy to accept the view that through one man's fault a nation will come under the punishments of God?

1 Chron 22:2–5. Collecting materials

In this section we see the immediate cause of David's census. He needed to know how many men could be made available for the work of quarrying the stone blocks for the fabric and, later, for the actual erecting of the building. It would not have done, of course, for the Chronicler to have connected the census which brought about the plague with the temple. The two parts of the story are kept apart. The point of this section is that the Chronicler is now able to state that David assembled enough men for the job.

(a) The stone was quarried by foreigners in forced labour gangs. It seems that the Chronicler could not face up to the fact that the kings were at times actually so forgetful of their own place and the dignity of Yahweh's folk as to include them in the corvee. The parallel passages in Samuel, the naming of the official who was in charge of the corvee (2 Sam 20:24), the reference to Solomon's corvee (1 Kg 5:13) and the stoning of Adoram at the beginning of Rehoboam's reign (1 Kg 12:18), all suggest that the corvee was certainly imposed on true Israelites as well as upon the aliens.

(b) The bronze collected here may be a heaping together of that paid in tribute by Betah and Berothai after the defeat of Hadadezer of Zobah (2 Sam 8:8) with the presents of Toi (cf 2 Sam 8:10).

(c) Cedar was bought from Hiram king of Tyre—perhaps David reserved to himself the use of some young trees in Hiram's woods when they should be full size. Solomon would then have claimed later what David had bought (cf 1 Kg 5:20 f). The text of Kings puts some emphasis on the skill of the Sidonians in the felling of trees.

(d) It is evident from 22:14 below that Solomon had still to collect wall-filling and scaffolding materials.

1 Chron 23:6–19. Instructions for the building

The charge to Solomon in 1 Kg 2:1–9 had included revenge clauses instructing the young king to pay off David's old scores against the men whom he had been for different reasons unable to kill himself. These clauses cannot be included in the Chronicler's version of the charge. For one thing it would bring out the carefully concealed curse on Joab, the leading man of the ideal knightly court, for another the reference to Shimei would lead the reader to curiosity about how Shimei came to be the enemy of David, and this would bring out the whole unhappy business of the revolt of Absalom. Most importantly, if Solomon performed the commands of his father, and it would be unthinkable that he should ignore such a charge, then he would be, like David, a man of blood, and the whole matter of the temple would be set back again through ritual impurity.

For the Chronicler 'the man of blood' was not only the warrior who fought for Yahweh, or the man who settled his private quarrels with a blow; either of these could be men of blood, but so could a host of others, for the designation was a liturgical one, referring to any who had contact with blood-letting in any situation. It was a designation of ritual impurity. Solomon must be kept from war and revenge and surgeons and all accidental bleedings or else the temple would never be built.

At this point the narrative is designed to perform a little editorial bridging. Just as the threshing floor incident moved the society from Gibeon to Jerusalem in the liturgical life, so the designation of Solomon as a man of peace is designed to indicate a new phase in the history of the covenant people. The Chronicler intends to bring the story from the old society of the Hebrew tribesmen who had no friends and no home settlements and who lived only in hope through Yahweh's promise to Abraham, to the new society of the Israelites in their country farmsteads and town houses, possessing the land and glorying in the wonder of the powerful political influence of the government in their city Jerusalem. The Chronicler had to accomplish this transition from exodus to city in terms which would maintain the continuity of the society as the people who were gathered by Yahweh. The building of the temple by Solomon is seen by the

Chronicler as the establishment of the old covenant values at the centre of the urban form of Israelite life.

The transition from David to Solomon is presented as a purification of the royal house so that it may come closer to the perfect service of Yahweh. The movement from David to Solomon is towards the building of the temple. History is determined by the liturgical demand of the people. Solomon succeeds because he comes nearer the ideal of covenant leadership than his father. And he comes nearer by conforming more closely to the demands of the cult.

The society has moved not into a radically different style of life but into a more perfect realisation of the demands of their old life. The pure young prince may bring the old holy vessels into the sanctuary.

The Chronicler had discarded Saul's family as irrelevant for his purpose when he was describing the opening of David's reign. He does not now clutter his account of Solomon's coming to power with any reference to those other sons who occupied the attention of the great historian of the Davidic succession narrative. Not for the Chronicler that sad tale of Adonijah's plot and the young prince's final killing. Everything about Solomon's accession has to be suited to the presentation of the king as 'the prince of peace'. Simply, the Chronicler says, David told all the princes of Israel to assist Solomon in the building of the great sanctuary.

1. Is our view of David affected by our knowledge that he wanted a full revenge upon his enemies and charged Solomon to deal with them?

2. Do we approve the Chronicler's simplification of David's character for his narrative purposes, or would we rather that he had shewn us the complexity of the man?

3

The temple—completion
1 Chron 23:1–2 Chron 9:31

1 Chron 23:1–27:34. Appointing the liturgical ministers

Levites (23:1–32, 24:20–31), priests (24:1–31), musicians (25:1–31), gate-keepers (25:1–28), treasurers (26:20–28) are carefully distinguished according to function and sub-divided according to family.

The whole interest of this set of genealogies, like that of the genealogies at the beginning of the story, derives from the urgency in the Chronicler's time of deciding just who was pure enough, in the cultic sense which had almost nothing to do with moral purity, to serve Yahweh in the restored liturgy. To appear in the lists was an essential basis for participation in the cult.

I saw lately a moderately interesting film about life in a British army camp of a brigade stationed in Africa. At one point a native politician declared to the regimental sergeant-major that his commanding officer had been killed and that he should now hand over the camp to the native government. The sergeant-major refused to accept this view of things, saying that he would only believe that the commander had been killed 'when I see it in the *Casualty Returns*'. The fact was not true until published in the list. The Chronicler would have accepted the sergeant-major's view. The native politician, by the way, did not. He was a revolutionary and did not share the Chronicler's and sergeant-major's concern with legitimate authority and the forms of tradition.

The Chronicler understood it to be a necessary public service to present a list of the cultic families so that anyone could check a man's claim to take part, either as a member of the congregation or as a minister in the sanctuary, in the covenant liturgy. The structure of society was not so secure that men could be allowed to rise by the whim of merit. If a ball is to bounce a wall is required. The Chronicler and his friends were busy building the wall and could not deal with the bouncing individual yet.

It is interesting to note that the men who minister in the sanctuary have now come to be regarded as personal servants of the master of the house. The levites and the other cultic persons are like household officials of Yahweh, attending to his domestic arrangements. The temple is now decidedly the house of Yahweh.

'Yahweh, the God of Israel, has given peace to his people; and he dwells in Jerusalem for ever' (1 Chron 23:25). The Chronicler has gone considerably further in this than the Deuteronomist allowed himself, and he has gone quite against the view of Jeremiah and his circle who disapproved of any circumscribing of Yahweh's presence in Israel.

The effect of the listing of David's civil and military arrangements is to enhance the notion of Yahweh as a squire in his manor-house. It becomes clearer and clearer to the reader of 36:29–32 and 27:1–34 that Yahweh is thought to run a household just like that of David. Retainers to look after the cooking, to keep the doors open for friends and barred against aliens, to provide musical entertainment, and to see to the domestic animals and the gardens, are required by both Yahweh and the king. This parallel set up by the Chronicler between Yahweh's estate and the royal court leads the reader to the thought that, if servants derive their dignity from the status of their master, then the priests and levites are obviously more important than the generals and the courtly scribes.

There is no moment in the Chronicler's history which is not employed for the forwarding of his main theme. The levitical cult forms the centre of the good society. The deuteronomist historian had used the temple liturgy as a standard of orthodoxy: he who worshipped in the high place was manifestly heretical. The Chronicler understands the Jerusalem liturgy as a standard of living, a vitalising force which makes sense of the institutional elements of Israelite society. He who shares in the cult shares in the best life.

1 Chron 28:1–21. The plans

The position David claims for himself and for Solomon is not one of simple hereditary right. Jesse's eldest son, or David's, might well have demanded the kingship if that had been the criterion of possession. Reality was quite contrariwise. Yahweh's choice of a man gives him authority among the people. And only Yahweh's choice can give such authority because the people are his people. The covenant is the primary reality of Israelite society and a king, if he is to make anything at all of his life, must accept the covenant as the sphere within which he can act.

Despite some distinguished commentators who have read the text of 1 Chronicles in a different sense, I think it quite clear that the Chronicler was determined that nothing, not even the Davidic royal household, should displace the free gift of Yahweh's covenant grace to his folk from the central position in the narrative. What David hands over to Solomon is not a sceptre of human rule, but a responsibility to fulfil the design of Yahweh's temple. David hands over the plans of the sanctuary, the regulations he has devised for the functions and numbers of the ministers, and the inventory of the sacred vessels. Royalty as it is presented in this succession narrative is itself a service of the cult.

It is to be noticed that the Chronicler has here quite departed from the account of the events as he found it in the work of the Deuteronomist in two major matters:

(a) In 1 Kg 1 the final glory for David is described as his being allowed to witness the establishment of Solomon as co-regent in Jerusalem.
(b) In 1 Kg 5 and 6 Solomon is credited with the planning of the temple and the arrangement of the cult.

In putting the cultic charge at the centre of his narrative the Chronicler has made certain that the liturgy and not the throne has been properly assessed by the reader as the prime institution in the community. In putting the temple arrangements at this point he has made the cult the principle of continuity which sustains the throne. Solomon is seen to be king because he is performing the kingly function of maintaining the liturgical impulse which had been given to the community.

Further, in the last of David's speeches to Solomon, 28:20–21, the Chronicler has placed phrases from the Deuteronomist's account of Moses (cf Deut 31:6 and 8; Jos 1:5), and he has thus established Solomon in a charismatic and not an hereditary leadership of the people.

1. Is there anything intrinsically more interesting in political or economic history than in the tracing of cultic traditions?

2. Is it proper to apply the terms of charismatic leadership to modern political presidents and party leaders?

1 Chron 29:1–30. Continuing expenses

The workmen had to be paid and the cultic persons too, the fabric had to be maintained, and the ceremonies continued in full splendour. David is certainly a man of practical business sense and he foresees what all his plans will cost in day-to-day expenses. He arranges a fund-raising drive among the richer men of the kingdom.

David's last speech to the assembled leaders is only cursorily concerned with the securing of Solomon on the throne and almost wholly devoted to assuring the success of the king's plans for the temple. The Chronicler presents David himself as subordinating royal succession to the great matter of the liturgy.

The presentation of the results of the fund-raising and their assignment to the temple project is the occasion of the final prayer of praise that David offers to Yahweh (29:10–20). And the prayer is offered to the God of Abraham, Isaac and Israel (another name for Jacob), that is to the God of the fathers. At his death David announced again the great covenant theme of the Chronicler's view of the community.

The accession of Solomon here, but not in the Kings account, is accompanied by the offering of sacrifice to Yahweh and, again without any worry of going against the Deuteronomist's version of the events, the whole community, including David's other sons, is said to have been brought together in harmony at the burnt offering.

A similar emphasis on the coming together of all elements of Israelite society is present in the final summary of David's reign (29: 26–30) in which the reader is given the impression that the king ruled 'all Israel' for forty years.

2 Chron 1:1–17. The builder

The Chronicler begins his account of Solomon with the king's address to 'all Israel', and his pilgrimage 'with the whole congregation' to the shrine at Gibeon. The list of the representatives of Israel who came to this meeting is set out as a parallel to the list of the representatives at the meeting called by Joshua at Shechem (Jos 24: 1).

The Chronicler is careful to protect the dignity of Jerusalem as the shrine of the ark and to prevent any surmise by an unorthodox Israelite that because Solomon made the first pilgrimage of his reign to Gibeon this shrine was the more important sanctuary. Gibeon, surrendering its place in Deuteronomist history as the greatest of all the shrines (cf 1 Kg 3:4), is here a station on the way to the temple. And the Chronicler has also turned the private prayer of Solomon at the shrine into a national meeting attended by the whole congregation. He does not want prayer to be esteemed a private royal occupation.

Solomon returns to Jerusalem. The Chronicler spends very little effort in the description of the king's personal virtues. The famous wisdom is not of interest to him, so the story of the harlots and the baby is quite left out. And Solomon's wealth is also not given the vulgar praise that the Deuteronomist historian lavished upon it as a sign of Yahweh's grace to the king. The main drive of the Chronicler's narrative is to present Solomon simply as the builder of the temple. The second, third and fourth chapters of 2 Chronicles are devoted to an account of Solomon's supervision of the temple building, and his care for the demands of the liturgy.

Four years having passed since Solomon's accession, chariots having been stationed at the barrack-cities of the kingdom, and the import-export trade in horses having been established, defence and money, that is, being secure, Solomon set about turning the blue-prints David had given him into grand buildings.

The Chronicler balances his emphasis on the building with an admission that no temple can suffice for Yahweh. Jeremiah had not preached quite in vain. The temple is not to contain Yahweh but to house his liturgical servants and provide a context for the liturgical meeting of Yahweh with his people. The temple is the focal point of a worship offered to the Lord who makes himself present.

1. How do we define the relation between the church building and God?

2. What place has the pilgrimage to a shrine—like Lourdes or Wagner's grave—in modern ways of thought?

2 Chron 2:1–5:1. The building itself

The Chronicler did not wish to spend much time describing an elaborate structure. His account is less fanciful and baroque than that of the Deuteronomist. This is probably because the Chronicler had no wish to arouse bitter regrets or vain wishes which would have debilitated those who came, after the exile, to worship in the less ornamented second temple. What remained of equal importance because of equal efficacy was the community worship. In that the second was no less than the first temple. The Chronicler therefore pays great attention to the liturgical prayer.

That the liturgy rather than the building is the source of continuity in the community is brought out by the Chronicler's strange assertion (not made anywhere before in the Jewish histories) that the site which Yahweh had selected for the temple was on Mount Moriah where Abraham had prepared to make a sacrifice of Isaac (Gen 22 : 2) and which was after that event 'the mount of Yahweh' (Gen. 22 : 14) and the site of prophetic wonder (cf Is 2 : 2, 30 : 29, 45 : 25, 46 : 20, Jo 3 : 17, Mic 4 : 1, Zech 8 : 3). The place had always been a context for Israel's prayer and Yahweh's gracious response.

The temple consisted of the *'ūlām* or portico, the *hēkāl* or main hall, and the *debīr* or sanctuary. Within the sanctuary stood the cherubs: winged animals, lions perhaps or bulls, with human heads. They may have been thought of as making a throne for Yahweh with their outstretched wings (cf 2 Sam 2 : 11) or as guardians of the ark (cf Gen 3 : 24). Like the whole temple complex of ornament and furniture, these creatures were fetched for new Jewish purposes by pagan craftsmen and received without any worry about idol-worship by the Israelites.

That the Chronicler, however, was aware of the likeness of the temple decoration to pagan models of the divine world, appears in his careful reference to 'something like oxen' (4 : 3) and his refusal to specify the symbolic decoration on the bronze stands (cf 1 Kg 7 : 27–39). There is no mention in 1 Kings of a curtain between the *hēkāl* and the *debīr*. Perhaps the first temple had doors (1 Kg 6 : 31) and the second, like the third, had a curtain there (cf Josephus, *Wars* v, 5).

For some account of Jachin and Boaz, the free-standing pillars to the right and left of the temple, have a look at the appropriate section of the commentary on 1 Kings

in this series (Vol 3, pp 128 ff)—also for something on
the 'bronze sea' and the unlikelihood of a basin con-
taining three thousand baths of water being employed
by the priests for hand-washing, 4:6 (a 'bath' equals
rather more than six gallons). The oxen under the basin
may represent the twelve tribes as they sat round the
tabernacle in the desert (cf Num 2), and certainly they
would be likely to make any Israelite think of the tribes
by their very number.

If the oxen were part of a reliable memory of the first
temple, the two courts of 2 Chron 4:9 certainly are not.
The two courts of 1 Kg 6:36 and 7:12 are a space next
to the temple and the whole of Solomon's built-up area,
but these two courts of the Chronicler are the general
fore-court of the temple itself and the inner court for
those who were ritually clean. These belong to the
second temple and have been read back into the first.

2 Chron 5:2–7:10. The dedication

The central act of the dedication ceremonies is the bringing, by the covenant community of 'all Israel', of the ark
to the *debīr*. For the last time the levites carry the ark to
its staying place. The scene is the climax of all those
carryings in the desert, across the Jordan, to Bethel,
Shiloh, Kiriath-jearim (which may have been another
name for Gibeon) and, at the Davidic festival procession,
to Jerusalem.

Together with the ark, the procession brings the tent
of meeting to the Jerusalem temple. It would seem that
Solomon's inaugural pilgrimage was the last event of
any moment to take place at the Gibeon shrine. After
that the Jerusalem shrine possessed every sacred sign
that the Israelites had preserved from their exodus journey. The procession of the ark and its attendant cultic

objects is obviously as important to the Chronicler as the procession David organised. The account in 1 Kg 8: 10 is elaborated at 2 Chron 5: 11–14 so that the procession with its great number of ministers will be the more significant.

The ark is now the visible centre of the community again, and the glory of Yahweh is among his people as before in the cloud of the exodus journey (Ex 13: 21–22), above the tent (Num 9: 15 ff), and so all manner of thing shall be well.

The dedication prayer. The stress here is on Jerusalem as the only city in which the liturgy, and particularly the sacrifice, is offered legitimately to Yahweh. It is not on Jerusalem as the home of Yahweh. The house is for 'the *name* of Yahweh' (6: 5, 7, 10, 20 etc), it is the place where his love and power are localised, but not the place where he is. The Chronicler insists throughout this prayer that Yahweh is 'in heaven' and hears 'from heaven' (6: 21, 23, 25, 27, 30, 33, 35, 39), and he repeats the thought expressed by David (in 1 Chron 28: 2 ff), that no building can house Yahweh since the highest heavens cannot contain him (cf 2 Chron 6: 18).

The temple is the place of worship and petition. The seven-part petition of 6: 22–39 is concerned with the happiness and security of the whole people and not the king alone. A quick analysis shows the petition to be made up from two sets of prayers:

1. (a) 22, sins against neighbours and the taking of oaths;
   (b) 24, sins in the community which prevent the national army obtaining victories;
   (c) 26, sins which prevent the coming of rain and the fertility of the fields;
   (d) 28, sins which bring famine or plague upon the whole people;

2. (e) 32, the prayer of the foreigner to be answered as
    a sign of the greatness of Israel's God;

   (f) 34, prayer for victory;

   (g) 36 f, prayer that repentant sinners should not be
    abandoned in exile.

Obviously the last of these petitions, and probably the
last three, which are cast in a different form from the
first four, and indicate a universalist outlook, and a time
when prayer was said facing Jerusalem, were added later
to the record made by those who took part in the original
event. The annals have been made to speak to the needs
of the Chronicler's contemporaries. The Chronicler has
added to the Deuteronomist's version of the event (which
he generally shortens) quotations from Ps 132 and Is 55.
It may be that we see here a fragment of the dedication
service of the second temple by Zerubbabel.

2 Chron 7:1. Yahweh authenticates the temple sacrifice
as he had that of the primitive Jerusalem sanctuary of
David (1 Chron 26:26), and the glory of Yahweh comes
spreading out from the *debīr* into the whole temple.

The people at this point sing the responses of Ps 136;
doubtless they are given here another piece of the Zerubbabel dedication ceremony to proclaim.

2 Chron 7:8. Solomon is surrounded for the further
feast of tabernacles by 'all Israel' who had come up from
all over the holy land, and who at the end of the feast
'went back to their tents'. The Chronicler is using ex-
pressions which although dying out of the language in
his own time bring out the covenant character of the
event, and remind men of the desert wonder.

1. How does the Chronicler's concept of Yahweh's presence in the liturgy connect with the doctrine of the real presence of Christ in the eucharist?

2. Is there ever a legitimate time for the invention of a 'tradition' in a society?

3. What service is done a community by the retelling of its early history?

2 Chron 7:11–9:31. The acceptance of the work

That Gibeon's whole claim to be a shrine of Yahweh is taken over by Jerusalem in the Chronicler's estimate is evidenced in the next incident which completes the temple narrative.

The tent of meeting having been brought to Jerusalem, Solomon is granted another vision of Yahweh, and this time in the great sanctuary itself. A sign that this vision story is an ancient tradition is that the revelation Yahweh makes to Solomon corresponds to only the (c) and (d) elements of the dedication prayer. This suggests that these two were probably the original components of the prayer and that all other elements are accretions, probably through a transference of ideas from the Zerubbabel dedication prayer.

The concentration upon rains, fields, and famine in the prayer and the response of Yahweh, together with the autumn character of the feast of tabernacles lends to the whole of the celebration following the dedication of the temple a fertility emphasis.

The second half of Yahweh's response is a firm refusal to put divine power into the command of man. Yahweh does not choose Solomon for better or worse. The nation itself does not have a claim to possess Yahweh. The Chronicler makes sure that the covenant (a term he employs here in 7:18 where the parallel in 1 Kg 9:5 has simply 'promise') is understood as a call to responsibility, and cannot be used to cover sin or apostasy. It is not an escape into favouritism.

The Chronicler's understanding of the covenant allows him to place responsibility for the destruction of the first temple wholly upon men. The temple fell not because Yahweh was weak but, quite contrariwise, because Yahweh was strong enough not to be infatuated with Israel. The temple was a sign of love not of doting. The collapse of the temple is not a reproach to Yahweh for being unable to protect himself but to Israel for supposing that Yahweh had been pocketed.

The Chronicler, in his account of the spring-time of the Jerusalem cult, points out that Solomon had the liturgical sense to appreciate that his queen was likely enough to be almost perpetually in a state of ritual impurity. He therefore removed her to a separate complex of buildings which did not have a connecting passageway to the temple itself. The kind of sensitivity evidenced here led Solomon's successor in the designing of the third temple to set up a separate 'court of the women'.

2 Chron 8:15. The ritual is always obeyed. 'They did not deviate in anything'. And with the performance of the ritual the work of Solomon is completed:

> And all Solomon's work which, until the day when the foundations of the temple of Yahweh were laid, had been only in preparation, was completed when the temple of Yahweh was finished.

For the rest of his life Solomon was really in retirement. He lived as a man should who has done a great work. He was prosperous and honoured, and did nothing that the Chronicler really thought worth setting down.

1. What place have visions in our general view of God's revelation of himself to men?

2. Are there elements in present christian attitudes which correspond to the Israelites' view that they had Yahweh in their pocket?

4
A succession of kings
2 Chron 10:1–28:27

2 Chron 10:1–12:16. Rehoboam

At Shechem, the old amphictyonic shrine, 'All Israel' is to concur in Rehoboam's becoming Yahweh's royal representative in the community, but a new leader comes, like Moses, 'out of Egypt'. Jeroboam and 'all Israel' ask that their right as free men of the covenant be respected.

And on the refusal of Rehoboam to acknowledge the covenant relation the people return 'to their tents', and, like those who had offended against the covenant in the time of Joshua (cf Jos 7:25), Adoram is stoned to death by the people. The Chronicler does not, however, think that the northern men breaking away from Rehoboam have brought about the destruction of the covenant community's effectiveness. The word of Shemaiah, the man of God, while referring to the northern men as 'your brothers', is addressed to Rehoboam and 'all Israel in Judah and Benjamin'. The promise and the covenant continue unbroken in southern loyalist tribes. The Chronicler thinks of the unity of Israel surviving the loss of the northern tribes rather as some Roman catholic theologians think of the unity of the christian church as unaffected by the refusal of orthodox and protestant churchmen to acknowledge the authority of the papacy.

Certainly the liturgical life was still to be discovered in Jerusalem, and the Chronicler thought that liturgical celebration enough to locate the true covenant people. As far as he was concerned the life of the community was still to be described as a circle and not an ellipse. The orthodox priests and levites from all over the country, north and south, come to serve in the capital city, while Jeroboam and his sons (over a long period) appoint upstart ministers of the cult who have no genealogy to their name.

To the Deuteronomist's malignant interpretation of the cherubim of Bethel and Dan, and his invention of the 'golden calf' story for the exodus saga, which suggested that Jeroboam, like the wicked men of the journey, had returned to the worship of Egyptian gods, to all this the Chronicler added the suggestion of the northerners worshipping 'the hairy ones'. He may be referring to the old country cults of the spirits of the hills, but more probably his condemnation, like the veto in Lev 17:5, is issued against the new worship of goat-demons at a Jerusalem city-gate (cf the suppression of this cult by King Josiah, 2 Kg 23:8) during the late pre-exilic age, and its revival after 587 in derelict towns where the goat-demons were thought to be the gods of the ruins (cf Is 13:21 and 34:12 and 14). The Chronicler is accusing the old northerners of practices characteristic of his southern contemporaries.

Purity of cult was however threatened not only in the north, even in the days of Rehoboam. Even if 11:23b is translated without any reference to the gods of Rehoboam's wives, 12:1 certainly condemns the king and 'all Israel' (that is, Judah and Benjamin as the new reality of Israel) as abandoning the observance of the law. The Chronicler is recalling the Mosaic past as the standard for the present community. And when the covenant people turn from Yahweh who brought them out of Egypt, then Yahweh brings Egypt to the very gate of Jerusalem. This theological point is made precisely through a piece of historical research, for at 2 Chron 12:2 the Chronicler has presented a far more detailed account of this important episode than that offered by the Deuteronomist in 1 Kg 14. The Chronicler's account has lately been corroborated by archaeological evidence of what was going on in the XXII dynasty.

Shishak's conquest-lists do not contain the name of Jerusalem among his conquered cities. The Chronicler explains how it was that the Egyptian invader failed to take the capital: Rehoboam and the leaders of Israel returned to the law. All that went to the conqueror was the golden panoply of the royal treasury. Perhaps the Chronicler's source for the Egyptian invasion was some fragment of an admiring account of Shemaiah, kept by one of his disciples (cf 12:15).

1. What relevance has a consideration of the Chronicler's view of the continuing unity of Israel to our own oecumenical considerations?

2. Could a religion survive the cessation of its liturgy once its devotees had been taught the necessity of corporate worship?

2 Chron 13:1–22. Abijah

This is a king after the Chronicler's heart. He glories only in 'the covenant of salt' (13:5) that Yahweh has made with him. Abijah, that is, fulfils the ritual of Lev 2:13, and obeys the cultic rules.

The Chronicler has evidently accepted a tradition

much more favourable to Abijah than that known to the Deuteronomist. Abijah's speech is set out by the Chronicler; it is of course his own invention, as a levitical sermon to the men of the post-exilic era. The king is said to have taken it as basic to a proper understanding of the royal task, that he, the Jerusalem king, should address 'all Israel'. He makes it clear that the king in Jerusalem rules as Yahweh's viceroy and from his viceregality derives his character as authoritative leader. As viceroy he enjoys the might of Yahweh. He cannot be resisted in battle.

More importantly, the king's prayers are offered in the true cult of the temple among the priests and levites of the exodus tradition, while the northerners are reduced to worship in a jumped-up liturgy at Bethel and Dan. There can be no question that the Jerusalem king's prayers will have a more favourable hearing than any offered at those unauthorised shrines. The battle is already decided for it is the holy war of Yahweh.

Abijah likens the camp of Jeroboam to Jericho. The priests are ready with their trumpets. The Chronicler has memories too of the routing of Midian by Gideon and his shouting men. And perhaps the reference to a ten-year peace for the men of the covenant after Abijah's heroic life is a literary attempt to bring this king into the old covenant world of the Judges. For similar phrases occur after the accounts of Othniel (Jg 3:11), Ehud (Jg 3:30), and Deborah (Jg 5:31).

With his demonstration that victory belongs to Yahweh and those who perform his ritual, the Chronicler makes an appeal to the men of his own time, perhaps particularly to the Samaritans of the northern territory, that they give up their illegitimate rituals and their make-shift gods and submit themselves to the regular

liturgy of the Jerusalem shrine. He makes a further
appeal in his account of the reign of the reformer Asa.

2 Chron 14:1–16:14. Asa

The history of Asa in Chronicles is much more detailed
a piece of work than the notice of the king in the Deuteronomist's history. He is presented here as a thoroughly
good chap who worked continually for the purification
of the cult—breaking up the foreign altars, pulling down
the Masseboth phallic stones, and the shrines of the
Canaanite sea-goddess, Ashteroth, and urging a renewal
of the people's covenant commitment to the law.

Politically Asa seems to have been an astute man, concerned with building up defensive walls in a period of
peace, maintaining a standing army as a warning to any
foe who might hope to attack the prosperous citizens,
and inflicting heavy losses upon the too-daring Zerah.

The Chronicler attributes the defeat of the Ethiopians
at Mareshah not to Asa and his political care for the
country but to the favour of Yahweh who was with the
king because of his loyalty to the cult. This piece of history is peculiar to the Chronicler and may have been
found by him in the records of the army high command.
The importance of such military facts lay, for the Chronicler, not in their historical character but in their further
demonstration of Yahweh's presence among his people.

Asa is said to have been supported by a seer (15: 1 and
8), and to have made an appeal to the northerners to
return to the central cult (15: 9). The Chronicler pays
special attention to the covenant renewal ceremony
(15: 12) which was celebrated like the Joshua renewal
at Shechem (Jos 24) and was followed, of course, by a
period of peace.

15:16 suggests that Asa's mother, the worshipper of the sea-goddess, was called Maacah. This opens out into an interesting difficulty in the text.

The reception of Bathsheba when she came to ask Solomon for a wife for Adonijah (1 Kg 1:19) shows how the Deuteronomist thought the queen-mother would be honoured by the king, and the importance of the queen-mother in the Chronicler's estimate is reflected in his reference to Naamah, 12:13, and his introduction to the reign of Abijah of Judah.

In that introduction Abijah's mother is said to have been the lady Micaiah, 13:2. 1 Kg 15:2, however, and 2 Chron 11:20 suggest that Abijah was the son of Maacah. Something has gone wrong here. The immediate conclusion must be that some ancient copyist has fallen asleep for a moment. But when 2 Chron 11:22 says that Maacah was the daughter of Absalom (not the princely son of David), and 2 Chron 13:2 that Micaiah was the daughter of Uriel, something more than a copyist's error is demanded to explain the texts and their ladies. And the demand becomes more urgent when it is noted that Abijah's successor, Asa, is said at 2 Chron 15:16 to have been the son of Maacah. Are we forced to suppose that all kinds of in-breeding have taken place in the royal homes? Is the Chronicler again dealing with something out of Hardy's Wessex?

Perhaps it should be allowed that Maacah was the mother of Abijah and received so great a reverence at the king's court that her immemorial authority and unofficial influence continued after her son's death and her grandson's accession. Perhaps the young Asa had been brought up in so strict an awe of the old lady that it took him some time before he could summon up enough

courage to depose his grandmother from her influence
and make his mother Micaiah chief lady of the court.

The interest of this incident for those who would understand the Chronicler's attitude towards all his
material is that it has been made to bear a theological
motive. The old lady's strength of character may have
kept her in power but the Chronicler suggests that she
came to the limit of her influence the moment that she
went off into the worship of strange gods. Her son gathered strength himself just when he had to defend the
purity of the cult in Jerusalem. Then 'at a stroke' the
idols are cut down. The Chronicler tells the story at this
moment with the relish of a small child recounting the
push that young Hansel gave the witch to topple her
into the oven.

Asa's prosperous Jerusalem appears to have been
highly attractive to the northerners. Perhaps they came
to shop as well as to worship. At any rate Baasha of Israel
realised that he was suffering in the comparison with the
king in the south. He therefore fortified Ramah and cut
off the roads to Jerusalem which was ten miles to the
south of this border town.

Asa, as a reprisal for the interruption of traffic, paid
the Damascus king to make trouble on the northern
border of Judah so that Baasha would have to abandon
Ramah to deal with the nuisance. When Baasha withdrew Asa rushed in and occupied the whole border territory.

Such humanly political activity could not be regarded
by the Chronicler as wholly laudable. Contrariwise. He
sees in the second half of Asa's reign a decadence from
the wonder of the reform era. The seer Hanani expresses
the Chronicler's disgust that money should be spent buying the services of foreign armies by a man who could

have lived under Yahweh's protection, and his shock that the king who had known how loving Yahweh could be to those who serve him, should consult physicians about his dropsical foot. Of course the king dies.

That the kingdom had to be always under the conditions of reform appears in this decadence of Asa after such a promising opening to the reign, and in the history of his successor, Jehoshaphat.

1. Does our society contain any relic of the old matriarchal manners?

2. What view do we have of the connection between prayer and cure of physical ills? Or of any ills at all?

2 Chron 17:1–20:37. Jehoshaphat

The young king faced a people who had quickly gone back to the fertility cults of the hill sanctuaries when Asa's reform movement had lost its drive during the military crisis. Jehoshaphat's response to the religious situation was to send the priests and levites with a suitably armed escort to the country towns to teach the people the full demands of Yahweh's law.

By making this favourable account of the young Jehoshaphat the Chronicler is deliberately setting himself against the Deuteronomist's thesis that there was no religious reform until the seventh century. It would certainly seem that the kings would, for merely political reasons if for no other, have wished to centralise the cult in their city of Jerusalem. So the Chronicler is probably correct in suggesting that several kings of the ninth century made efforts to suppress the fertility sanctuaries.

That the Chronicler was not inventing the Jehoshaphat effort for Yahwism seems to be supported by evidence from the account of the mission to the cities of Judah in which the laymen are listed before the clerics. The Chronicler seems here to be relying on an old source for his information, for he would certainly have placed the levites first in the story if he had been inventing it. Perhaps indeed the Chronicler is using a military record for most of this chapter, possibly from the same archives as his information about the defeat of the Ethiopians at Mareshah, and perhaps, further, he has inserted 17:8 into this military record to make it appear that the priests and levites had a proper share in the suppression of the country shrines. The new king may have relied entirely upon military officers to eradicate the centres as possible meeting places for grousing subjects. 'The book of the law of Yahweh' may not have been a version of the priestly Pentateuch but rather a set of royal enactments for the quiet of the realm. The Chronicler was quite capable of canonising a rather secular activity in his account of how things were once.

At any rate the message is clear: once Yahweh was obeyed in the realm other nations would see the resulting prosperity and they would be brought to honour Yahweh and bring tribute to his viceroy in Jerusalem. Such a king would not need marriage allowances to secure his borders or to prop up his economic policies. The Chronicler is highly critical of the alliance with Ahab and tells the tale, although its action takes place in the northern kingdom with which he generally has little business, to show how useless such an alliance must prove.

Jehoshaphat maintains his Yahwism in the northern kingdom at least so far as to ask that the elder king of the north call for the prophet Micaiah after he has heard the royal prophets of Ahab. It is this remnant of proper loyalty to Yahweh in the situation which brings the young king off unharmed from the battle in which Ahab dies. 'Yahweh helped him' (18:31).

Lest we miss the point of the previous narrative Jehu the seer is brought to meet Jehoshaphat on his way home to Jerusalem. He makes it plain that the alliance is no good and that Jehoshaphat has only been rescued from death because his previous service of Yahweh outweighed his present folly.

The picture that the Chronicler gives of this reign is quite idyllic. The king walks among his people, instructing them in the law of Yahweh, ensuring justice in the courts, seeing that the liturgy is properly performed, and religious disputes quickly settled.

Little is said of Jehoshaphat in the Deuteronomist's history because that historian was mightily concerned with the activities of Elijah and Elisha in the northern kingdom, and so wrote more about Ahab and the north at this period. But even in the Deuteronomist's history there are pointers to Jehoshaphat being a good king who worked for a peaceful society in the south (cf 1 Kg 22, 2 Kg 3 and especially 2 Kg 3:14).

The episode of the Moabite attack is conducted on properly Yahwistic lines. The pagan enemy is announced as humanly horrifying, so horrifying that the king orders a community fast and a community prayer in Jerusalem, himself leading the people in the invocation of Yahweh. The prayer lays stress on Yahweh as Lord of the world, he is not a local god to be chased from his local sanctuary, he can deal with every army which comes against his shrine. The prayer is backed by a reference to the covenant promise and the exodus saga.

Yahweh replies to the prayer through the levite of proven family: 'You will not need to fight. See what Yahweh will do for your salvation'. And the king on the battle day pledges his loyalty to the word and promise of Yahweh. The battle therefore becomes a holy war event.

The battle line is led by the levitical singers in the linen robes that they wore in the Jerusalem liturgy. The enemy are thrown into such confusion that, like those Midianites who woke to the trumpets of Gideon, they strike out wildly and kill each other.

Then the men of Judah gather the booty at their leisure and take it first to the ritual assembly on the battlefield, and then, in procession, to Jerusalem with the levites leading them in hymns of praise for Yahweh. The temple's financial requirements here, as before, alter the conditions of the holy war. There is no ban here because there is an alternative way of dedicating the booty to Yahweh. To hand it over to the priestly ministers of the temple was thought to be taking it out of the hands of men, at least it was thought so by the Chronicler.

1. Both the Deuteronomist and the Chronicler felt it their proper business to make the shape of history manifest. Do we now suppose that history has any shape other than in the mind of the historian?

2. What kinds of holy war or crusade obtain popular support today? Is it possible, for example, to give a theological interpretation of the various programmes of the conservationists?

2 Chron 21:1-24:27. Jehoram and others

The reign of Jehoshaphat is highlighted against the darkness of the reign of his son, Jehoram, which begins in a series of murders, continues in a marriage alliance with the heretical north, a set of military disasters, religious apostasy on the hillsides, and perhaps even in the city of Jerusalem itself, and ends in the invasion of the country by an enemy, the killing of the king's family, his own death in utmost agony from some dreadful disease, and his burial in a grave apart from his Davidic ancestors.

To this chaos the citizens of Jerusalem attempted to give some shape. They made the young Ahaziah (Jehoahaz) king under the regency of the queen-mother Athaliah who belonged to the ruling family of Israel. Her influence on the life of the city and the court was such that it became indistinguishable in wickedness from the northern capital and there followed an alliance between north and south against Hazael.

In the fight Jehoram of Israel was wounded and while he was convalescing he was visited by the young Jerusalem king. So far the Deuteronomist and the Chronicler agree. Each has, however, his own ending to the story. The Chronicler says that after Jehu, the man of vengeance sent by Yahweh, had killed Jehoram of Israel, he sent his soldiers to search for the southern king, and on winkling him out from a hiding-place in Samaria, had him put to death and buried. The Deuteronomist's story of the young king being pursued in a chariot race across the plain and coming with a death-wound in his back to Megiddo, ends with the body of the king being sent back to the south for burial.

The Deuteronomist's tale is certainly the more exciting but there is no reason to suppose that it is the version with greater historical value. The Chronicler often seems to be more reliable than the Deuteronomist when the two are confronted with archaeological checks. There is as yet no way of telling which had the facts straight on this occasion.

On the death of the king her son, Athaliah had her

whole family assassinated so that she might have all power in the kingdom. She ruled wilfully and wickedly for six years, but on the seventh, as in every good story, rescue arrived with the appearance of a young boy at the centre of a temple counter-plot.

The clerics called for help from the army commanders and these set about gathering support in the country generally. They arranged a meeting of priests, generals, and manorial squires in Jerusalem at which they all took an oath to secure the return of Yahweh's rule in the country. Jehoiada, the priest, who had, with his wife the princess Jehoshabeath, looked after Ahaziah's baby son, Joash, quickly saw to the practical details of the coup and (here again the Chronicler departs from the better-known Deuteronomist's version of the plot) ensured that the military in their counter-revolutionary zeal did not violate the sanctity of the temple. He armed the levites and the temple guards, keeping the purely army men on the temple steps to control the crowd. Then the young prince was led in and surrounded by the levitical orders, Joash was anointed by Jehoiada and his priestly sons. Joash was now the king sent by Yahweh.

It is tempting to suppose that the boy was a prince from nowhere. It seems unlikely that so efficient a murderess as Athaliah would not have made sure that the baby was dead with the rest. There's an Anastasia-like problem here. Was the boy really Jehoahaz' son?

The temple was protected against blood pollution by the priest's insistence that Athaliah be killed outside the gate, and as the porters guarded the sacred threshold and the levites blew on their trumpets, the new reign began in proper ritual style with the affirmation of the covenant. This is followed immediately by the destruction of the Baal altar that Athaliah had had erected in the holy city for the usage of her northern friends when they came to court. The world of the law has returned.

The law returned as no respecter of persons. Joash thinks the levites a lazy lot who do not care enough for the upkeep of the Jerusalem shrine and who are not conscientious in the maintaining of the law's directions for the ritual. He tells Jehoiada to stir things up a little among his sanctuary attendants. His intervention is of course quite proper. Every member of the covenant community had the right and responsibility to ensure that the covenant was being taken seriously at all points of Israelite society. But it cannot have been pleasant for the priest to be taught his business by the boy he had reared and made king to serve his priestly purposes. And Joash struck at the very centre of the business by regulating the financial dealings of the priests.

A chest was placed in front of the temple to hold the dues demanded by the law of all who worshipped at the sanctuary. The proceeds were designed for the upkeep of the shrine but the king thought that this duty had been neglected by the priests and took upon himself the burden of cultic fabric. Surprisingly the Chronicler thinks he can get away with the comment that the people, who were now made to keep up their dues for the shrine, rejoiced at the renewal of the levy.

In the Deuteronomist's version of these events the financial affairs of the temple did not pick up. The clergy did not seem able to distinguish properly between essentials and inessentials, between the necessities of fabric affairs and the desirabilities of liturgical vessels. There is a hint too that the levites may have been quietly pocketing some of the money for their private uses. The Chronicler, however, passes in silence over such gossip about his levites. He stresses, instead, the continual observance of the sacred liturgy throughout Jehoiada's life, the great and honourable age of the priest at his death, his royal burial, and the collapse of the reform when the laymen got hold of the king.

Yahweh did not desert his folk on the death of the good old priest. He sent seers to recall the people to the liturgical life, and these doubtless are remembered because they were for a time successful in keeping the Yahwist faith alive, and for their final failure. For there came a moment when the king on Yahweh's throne ordered the killing of the son of Jehoiada, Zechariah the priest, in Yahweh's temple.

Yahweh is not mocked. In the days of Abijah (2 Chron 13:13 ff) and Asa (2 Chron 14:8 ff), Yahweh had shewn that with a few men he could put thousands to flight, now though Jerusalem has a great army a few Arameans are allowed to defeat the men of the southern kingdom, and a group of servants are allowed to assassinate the king himself (24:25) and to throw his body into a commoner's grave.

2 Chron 25:1–28. Amaziah

A pause at the beginning of Amaziah's reign for the legal disposal of the late king's murderers, and then downhill all the way. The census, the hiring of northern mercenaries, the erection of shrines for the captured gods of Seir, and threats against the prophet of Yahweh, lead finally to the demented pride of the challenge to Joash of Israel.

The confrontation of the two kingdoms ends in the defeat of Amaziah's army, his own capture, the sack of Jerusalem, of the temple itself, and at the last a hunted existence for the poor king who flees from town to town, afraid of his own soldiers as much as of the enemy's pursuer's, and finally cut down by his guardsmen.

2 Chron 26:1–27:9. Uzziah

This king inquires of Yahweh and obeys the Yahwist Zechariah, and is rewarded by victory and prosperity and fame. A pastoral idyll of cattle and corn and vines surrounds the newly built towers of topless Jerusalem, until the moment when Uzziah arrogantly takes to himself the priestly functions. Then everything changes. A king can get away with all sorts of things but he can never take over the levitical privileges. He is blasted with leprosy as he struts in the sanctuary. And his leprosy must have been of the most frightful kind, for, unlike Naaman who remained in command of an army (2 Kg 5), the king has to withdraw from public life.

That merely keeping out of the sanctuary and having military successes is not enough to stir the Chronicler's interest, however, is shewn by his off-hand account of Jotham.

2 Chron 28:1–27. Ahaz

In dramatic preparation for the great reforms of Hezekiah the Chronicler tells the tale of the infamous Ahaz who did nothing right. This king 'followed the ways of the kings of Israel'. Nothing worse could be said of him. All else that follows follows naturally from this description: the erection of Baal altars, the rituals of child sacrifice in the Gehenna valley and the fertility dances in the country groves, are signs of total apostasy.

And apostasy as usual leads to defeat, but, worse than usual, the king does not repent in his defeat, he continues to worship the gods of Damascus, he shut the temple and set up altars for the rites of strange gods in the holy city itself. The liturgy ceased. Nothing worse could happen in the life of the covenant community.

1. What arrangements would seem best to us for the financing of the church?

2. What, in our urban society, has taken the place of the pastoral dream of two acres and a cow—two cars and a swimming pool?

3. Does every society need its pagan carnivals?

5

The end of the line
2 Chron 29:1–36:23

2 Chron 29:1–30:27. Hezekiah

Hezekiah is the king who turns the balance of history against the wicked Amaziah. The Chronicler has taken the figures of Hezekiah's reign and fitted the figures of Amaziah to them so that when the reader arrives at the account of Hezekiah's reign he discovers a perfect counter to the earlier tale of royal wickedness. Thus the probably historically accurate statement of the king's age at his succession and the length of his reign, are pre-echoed in the most unlikely suggestion of a twenty-five-year-old Amaziah and his reign of twenty-nine years. The figures have been carefully arranged for a theological purpose.

Hezekiah became king in 715 and died in 687. On these facts, expressed in their own dating-system, the Deuteronomist and the Chronicler would probably, if they had been asked, agreed. They differed widely, however, in their assessment of the significance of what happened in that period. For the Deuteronomist the reform of Josiah was the great event of the history and Hezekiah was, therefore, to be appreciated simply as a forerunner of the greater king. The Chronicler was not impressed by any individual of the Davidic line. He lived late enough to judge what little lasting value there was in the Josiah reform. So he was not anxious to shew Heze-

kiah as preparing for anyone greater. The Chronicler
did have, of course, his own interests and his own view
of the shape of history. His experience determined his
selection and interpretation of events in the past and he
saw Hezekiah as a king whose story could teach his own
contemporaries a great deal about the meaning of Yahweh's covenant with the people.

Hezekiah is the man who did right. He opened the
doors of the temple and renewed the consecration of the
levites. The first act of the king is offered as proof of his
righteousness. His first speech shows that he has intelligence enough to appreciate the cause of Judah's military
failure and social chaos. He declares his intention of re-
newing the covenant world, and his confidence in the
levites as the men who can again arrange a ritual pleasing
to Yahweh.

The levites, of the proper families, of course, respond
to the king's invitation. Under his patronage a huge
ritual cleansing takes place. The ministers, the sanctuary, the vessels, are all made worthy once more of their
allotted parts in the covenant ritual.

Then the king arranges the bringing by the leaders of
the people of the necessary animals for the sin-offering.
The levites take up the sacred instruments, the king
orders the burnt offering to be made on behalf of 'the
whole congregation'. Atonement is effected and the community is once more sharing in the grace of Yahweh.
And being once again at one with each other and with
Yahweh, the people are encouraged to make a festival of
offerings to Yahweh. So great was the pressure of cultic
business, so many animals to be prepared, so many
prayers to be chanted, that the levites were given priestly
functions. The Chronicler at this point in his history has
found the justification of a contemporary practice. In

the Chronicler's day the levites were so much more faithful in the performance of their duties than the old
priestly families that the Chronicler wanted to show that
there was a precedent for turning over to the levites all
kinds of peculiarly sacerdotal functions.

After such a thanksgiving all was well in the realm
and Hezekiah could begin his work of uniting all those
who had a traditional share in the covenant. He sent
messages to the northern men to come to the Jerusalem
passover. From Dan to Beersheba the invitation was announced in the name of the God of the fathers (2 Chron
30:5).

Hezekiah was evidently making a political as well as
a religious effort to bring the men of the north under his
influence when he sent out the invitations to the passover celebrations. The Chronicler, however, was not
concerned with Hezekiah's power politics. He used the
incident to make a levitical sermon to men of his own
time that the scattered worshippers of Yahweh all over
Palestine should come together round the rebuilt sanctuary in Jerusalem.

Sermons. A great deal of the Chronicler's work is
written in the homiletic style of this section. It seems
likely that the Chronicler has inserted shortened versions of actual levitical sermons of his own day. He thus
increased the circulation of levitical ideas. Examples of
such sermons have been noted at various points in the
narrative, occurring in the mouths of prophets, levites
and kings, who all speak in the same accent, putting forward in solemn prose the fundamental beliefs of Israel
without much thought of the appropriateness of the
expression to any particular historical situation. The
general shape of these sermons derives from the post-
exilic preaching the Chronicler knew. He may have used

the very words declaimed at those gatherings organised by the levites who were travelling around the country in his own day recalling the folk to the old covenant responsibilities. The speeches he sets down are studded with quotations from the law and the prophets and the psalms which often shore up the argument simply by their high-sounding moralities rather than by perfect relevance to the situation being discussed. The language of these quotations gives a sense of antiquity and authority to the new sermon, rather as the language of Elizabethan translations of the bible is even now thought by some doormat conversionists to be proper for the modern English housewife, and by some clerical liturgists to be proper for new public prayers.

But the sermons are not simply intended to create a sense of ecclesiastical authority under the ritual law. The accusation of mere legalism which is so often made against the post-exilic community is not to be sustained by recourse to those sermons. They are evidently concerned with the great truths of Israel's faith, with the grace of Yahweh to the penitent, the justice of Yahweh and its vindication in history, the necessity of faith in Yahweh if the world is to make sense, and if the community is to have peace.

A nice example of such a sermon occurs in 2 Chron 15:2–7, when Azariah meets king Asa after the defeat of Zerah the Ethiopian. This sermon is held together by two quotations from the prophet Jeremiah (cf Jer 29:14 and 31:15) and deals not with the immediate results of victory but with the distresses of the period of the judges and the general truth that Yahweh will be found by those who seek him, and concludes with the exhortation to work for the divine reward. Evidently this sermon, which is typical, is based upon a religious faith rather more substantial than mere legalism.

Such sermons are put into the mouths of all kinds of folk. A levite has a sermon at 2 Chron 20:15, another is given to a seer, the man of Yahweh, at 2 Chron 25:7, and another to a messenger of Hezekiah at 2 Chron 30:6.

Not only holy men are given sermons to preach. King Jehoshaphat delivers a sermon to the judges of Judah (2 Chron 19:6 ff) on the administration of justice in a community whose justice must be the reflection of the justice of Yahweh. The king's speech is an elaboration of Deut 10:17 and Zeph 3:5 performed in just the way an experienced preacher might manage. The speech is a well-made piece of homiletics. This king, who was not I suppose any more preachy than other kings (Hezekiah preaches at 2 Chron 32:7 and David himself does it at 1 Chron 28:2) has a second sermon, though a particularly shortened one this time, at 2 Chron 20:20.

The Chronicler has evidently a greater interest in securing the true belief of his own contemporaries than in recording history 'as it happened'. He has no desire to set down anything so useless as a court annal or a king list. He thinks of history and the historian's task as a discipline of immediate 'relevance' to the condition of his own society. He is himself fulfilling, in his making of the record, his allotted work in the covenant situation of restored Jerusalem. Hezekiah's passover sermon is for the Chronicler a message to those in the surrounding countryside to abandon the Samaritan nonsenses and to come into the circle of the Jerusalem service. Some northerners, he points out, laughed in the past when such an invitation was made to them. Others came. Though some laugh in the present, the chance is that some others will come, and this chance must not be neglected.

So the Chronicler, 30:17, tells his readers that even those who were not ritually clean were welcomed into the holy community at this passover celebration. They were made clean by their coming.

From this new cleanliness of the folk there developed a renewal of the whole land, the destruction of the fertility figures, the over-turning of the hill shrines, even those over the border within the northern territory, and the whole ecclesiastical establishment was set up economically so that there would be no chance of the reform collapsing because of lack of funds and supplies. King and priest act together and the land is at peace with Yahweh. Obviously the Chronicler is concerned with the establishment of a similar concord of civil and ecclesiastical power in his own society.

The story of the Assyrian invasion illustrates the ultimate strength of such a society as that he has just described. Though the Assyrian came to the gates of Jerusalem he has to turn shamefacedly back to his own country. The people who held to their faith in Yahweh are thus held in honour among the nations (2 Chron 32).

1. Are there moments in contemporary society when it is generally thought that things can be cleaned up and started afresh? Could the new beginning ever be effected by political means?

2. Is there now in our churches a recognisable sermon style, or are sermons generally not expected to have a style?

2 Chron 31:1–21. The hill shrines

The pillars and sacred posts of 2 Chron 31:1 which are pulled down by the Israelites returning from the

Hezekiah passover celebration are signs of male and female Canaanite deities. These objects may have been first set up as commemorative steles, recording the place of a treaty or a theophany (cf, for example, the stone set up by Jacob after his vision at Bethel, Gen 28 : 18). They certainly ended up by being accepted as representations of the gods themselves, whether crude sculptural efforts had been made to render the pillars anthropomorphic or not.

The stone *massebah* was a sign of a god, the wooden *'asherah* that of a goddess, for it is a word made by a deliberate misvocalisation by the Hebrews to avoid saying the name of the hated goddess Astarte. The name is thus used both for the great goddess of the Canaanite fertility cults and for her representation, rather as a man might now say that he had lit a candle 'in front of Our Lady'.

The wooden post might be a living or dead tree but was generally set up by man on a hill-top or an artificial mound of earth that could equally well be called 'a high place', or even on a wooden platform in a town temple (cf 1 Kg 16 : 33 and 2 Kg 3 : 2). Perhaps the tree under which Adam and Eve first became aware of their sexuality is related to the *'asherah*. Certainly, in corroboration of this idea, the snake was a creature associated with the goddess in the Canaanite cults. It is possible that the whole cluster of effective images surrounding the Genesis account of the fall derives from what the Hebrews knew of the *'asherah* ritual and was employed in an orthodox effort to keep the Israelites away from the intriguing Canaanite ceremonies (look also at the command of Sinai, Ex 34 : 13 and Deut 16 : 21 f). The half-horrified and half-fascinated attitude of sophisticated folk to the Andean wood-rites displayed on television screens, and the turn of mind which allows Roman catholics to rehearse odd tales of the masonic ritual, are perhaps examples of the same forces at work in modern society.

The high places and their rituals were always a counter-attraction to the cult of Jerusalem, and both prophets and historians put in huge efforts to dissuade the people from going to the abominations that were celebrated in the shrines. That the condemnation of the high place and the pillar-cults occurs so frequently in the Israelite records is an indication of the ineffectiveness of the threats and ridicule that the orthodox employed against them. There were numerous times, indeed, when the Canaanite cults invaded Jerusalem and forced their way into the community liturgy. It is evident, for example, that Hezekiah would never have had the irreligious daring to throw out from the temple sanctuary the brazen serpent that had stood there for years if he had believed the story of Moses and the plague (2 Kg 18: 4 and Num 21 : 9). The tale was invented to make orthodox sense of such a thing's being in the sanctuary. The recent dig at Timna suggests a Midianite origin for this cult object.

1. What purpose is served by our public monuments, statues and cenotaphs?

2. How do we interpret the fall story for ourselves?

2 Chron 32:1–33:25. Sin, repentance and prayer

The splendid story in the Deuteronomist's narrative of Hezekiah's illness is cut to a quick sentence which says everything the Chronicler needs to take from the incident. That prayer can change everything because the power of Yahweh is without limit in time or space is a theme which recurs through the Chronicler's history (cf, for

example, 1 Chron 4: 10, 5: 20, and 2 Chron 15: 5, 32: 20)
and here Hezekiah is shewn as being recovered by
Yahweh from sickness and war because the king had
recourse to the prayer of a humble man. On this moral
note the history of one king is ended, and that of his son
continued for, quite against the Deuteronomist's version
of Manasseh's reign, the Chronicler has put at the end of
the catalogue of horrors an exiling of that king in chains
to Babylon, and a repentance there for all Manasseh's
earlier sin, a repentance which culminates, 33: 18, in his
prayer to Yahweh and his rebuilding of the walls of
Jerusalem.

The Deuteronomist knew nothing, evidently, of 'the
records of the kings of Israel' or 'the records of his seers'
which the Chronicler says are the sources for this repentance and prayer. The Chronicler was perhaps forced to
be more determined in his search for material to include
in his account of this reign, for he was forced to recognise
in Manasseh a particularly striking form of a problem
important for all Israelite historians.

The problem arose in the confrontation of Yahweh's
righteousness and man's sin. Divine punishment must
come upon the sinner. And for the Jew of the
Chronicler's time such punishment must come in this
life, for personal survival after death, and therefore the
possibility of personal reward or punishment after death,
was not yet part of the orthodox faith of the community.

The sinner must be punished in this life according to
a just divine law. So it must appear that ill-luck in
mercantile operations, disease, and death are signs of
Yahweh's law working out a just punishment for a man's
sins. Contrariwise, wealth, health, and long life, are
signs of Yahweh's rewarding a man for being good.

The theory reconciles Yahweh's power with the

various conditions of men. It requires of course that the community does not entertain any question as to Yahweh's fairness. There may be occasions when a man who seems good is getting rather a bad time of it in the market place or always suffering from gout, and the people must accept that the man is only appearing to be good while living a bad life. And when a bad man appears to prosper the community must accept that disaster is waiting for him round the corner. In order that this faithful acceptance of Yahweh's inexorable justice may be made with some conviction the Chronicler takes it to be his duty to show that the good, or the repentant, prosper and the bad suffer horribly.

When the Chronicler came to record the events of the reign of Manasseh he saw that the king had ruled for a very long time, and that, quite against the true story of history, he had ruled for that long time in a manner not at all in accord with the demands of the covenant. The Deuteronomist on being confronted with this sport in history had simply introduced a paragraph of threats into his narrative and hoped that the reader would assume that the king came to a bad end. The Chronicler thought that the situation required rather more than this to set it right. He took another look at the history to find the cause of Manasseh's longevity.

Perhaps Manasseh was involved in some conspiracy of Levantine city states against the Assyrian, and perhaps he was called to Nineveh by Ashurbanipal to explain his action. The facts however are of less importance than the theological truth that Yahweh has the power to enforce his will upon events. The Chronicler makes it clear that Manasseh's reign would have been properly short if the king had not repented. He was given a long life of rule

in Jerusalem as a reward for his return to the service of
Yahweh.

Manasseh, the bad man who had to be rather covered
up by the Deuteronomist is, by a bold stroke of the
Chronicler, made in total faith in the consistency of
Yahweh's will, turned into an example for all true men
of the covenant. Repentance will always be rewarded by
Yahweh. Turn back to Yahweh and all will be well.

To the Chronicler Manasseh must have seemed a
paradigm of his own community which had fallen into
sin, been punished by the exile, and come after prayer
to rebuild Jerusalem. The king was a sign for Israel.

The reign of Amon who would not pray shows to what
misery the unrepentant man must come.

2 Chron 34:1–35:26. Josiah

The reign of Josiah is recounted as a sign of prayer at
work. After the reign of Amon and the neglect of the
liturgy the destruction of the old shrines through the
land comes as a sign of the community's repentance. This
is stage one, described in 34 : 3–7.

Stage two is the preparation for a celebration of the
liturgy. 'All the remainder of Israel', both south and
north, are brought into the community work by the
missions of the travelling levites, 34 : 8–13.

Stage three is the reading of the law so that the community will know how it is to behave in the covenant.
The priest tells the king and the people what the demands
of the covenant mean for their lives, 34 : 14–30.

Stage four is the acceptance by the community of the
law's demands and the renewal of their pledge of loyalty
to Yahweh.

Repentance ends, as it must in the Chronicler's view,

if it is to be seen as real by men and Yahweh, with the
community participating in liturgical prayer. The passover is celebrated as if they were all beginning again;
as at the first festival ever held by their countrymen in
the city, the levites are told to put down the ark, though
it had been resting for centuries, the family posts are
assigned, and the Davidic arrangements for the singers
are repeated. The sense of newness is enhanced by the
declaration that 'there was not celebrated a passover like
it in Israel since the days of Samuel the prophet', and
the sense of community is made plain by the reference to
the presence of 'all Judah and Israel' (2 Chron 35 : 19).

*1. The Chronicler says very little about 'private
prayer'. Would we want him to say more? Is liturgical,
popular, corporate, prayer enough for us?*

*2. The Chronicler seems to be quite sure that he
knows what sort of society is the best, and he works for the
coming of that society. Do we share his certainty? Do we
have a clear idea of what we mean when we pray 'Thy
kingdom come'?*

2 Chron 36:1–23. The end

That the kings did not remain loyal to Josiah's repentance prayer allows the Chronicler to dismiss Jehoahaz,
Jehoiakim and Jehoiachin, as slippery slopes to the
catastrophe of Zedekiah, who was offered a chance for
repentance when Jeremiah preached in Jerusalem, and
refused his chance. Zedekiah took the chiefs of Judah
with him into the abyss of desecrating the temple,
ridiculing the messenger of Yahweh, and despising the
love of Yahweh. At the end the king is taken into exile,
the city is sacked and the temple destroyed.

But of course Yahweh is ever faithful, ever loving, ever mindful of the covenant. The last sentence of the account of Zedekiah's reign is one of hope. The course of that hope is made plain in Jer 25: 11 and Lev 26: 41–43. The Chronicler returns at the end to the form of the levitical sermon to make his point about the significance of the history. He is preaching from texts which his reader would recognise. And his sermon is concerned with the relation of sin and repentance and hope. He is making plain his belief that repentance will always bring the men of the covenant into Yahweh's good favour. The exile thus becomes a way of purgation for a new life.

The promise of Yahweh and the fulfilment of that promise remain, waiting on prayer. Yahweh is waiting for the renewal of the temple liturgy when his people will once more 'go up' to Jerusalem in happy pilgrimage. That this phrase remained the traditional term for taking part in the celebration of the liturgy in the temple, and was connected in Jewish minds with atonement and reconciliation, is plain from a reading of Jn 7: 8–10.

Ezra—Nehemiah

1
The edict of Cyrus
Ez 1:1–6:22

Ez 1:1–3:6. The gathering of Israel

Knitting his narrative to the end of 2 Chronicles in order
to give the appearance of chronological continuity, the
editor of our Ezra begins with the edict of Cyrus. The
Persian emperor made possible the celebration of the
Jerusalem liturgy and so set in motion the vital action
of the community. The reader is to appreciate that the
return to Jerusalem is not important for Israel primarily
as a political event. It takes its significance from the possibility it offered of a renewal of liturgical prayer in the
temple. The people are again 'to go up to Jerusalem', the
pilgrimage of 'all Israel' is to start again with songs and
dances, the march is to be made again into the promised
land.

    The Chronicler, like other Israelite writers of this
period (cf Is 41:17 ff, 43:16 ff, 48:21) thinks of the
return as a second exodus event and, while Cyrus may
have suggested that those prosperous Israelites who were
content to remain in comfortable exile should finance
the return of those who wished to go back to Judah, the
Chronicler has made out of Cyrus' edict an enforcement
upon the Babylonians themselves to pay for the journey.
The Babylonians, therefore, take the part of the old
Egyptians who were forced to give the escaping Hebrews

jewels and supplies for the march (Ex 3:21, 11:2–3, 12:35–36).

The tribesmen, the priests and the levites go singing towards Jerusalem carrying with them the sacred vessels that the wicked Babylonians had taken off for their wanton feastings. The Israelites are once again making the public pilgrimage to their shrine.

This is the beginning of a gathering of 'all Israel', and the Chronicler devotes a great section to his catalogue of virtuous families who took part in the procession. A second version of this liturgical listing occurs at Neh 7. The purpose of so much fussing about the family list has been disputed by commentators but it seems obvious that the Chronicler's motives here are exactly those he, or his final editor, had in making the first great historical list at the beginning of his entire work. The families, here as in the opening of 1 Chron, represent the race and give a sense of continuity with the men of the tribes who first enjoyed membership of the covenant. The community of the covenant is being re-established in Jerusalem and in his own time the Chronicler would be glad to point to the family list as an encouragement for the present generation to live up to the standards of their great ancestors.

Ez 2:59. The 'first families' contrast mightily with those unfortunates who were unable to prove their lineage, and who were therefore unable to claim a place in the liturgy.

That the Chronicler was quite representative of his folk in this serious delight in genealogies is shown by the assumption that even in the midst of the upheaving exile and return the lists of Israelite families were still kept up to date and consulted.

That the Chronicler was not, however, bound by the human records but appreciated that the specific distinction of Israel was the relation that the families had to Yahweh, appears in his setting down the governor's decision—apparently quite acceptable to the community —that if evidence was not available in the official records then Yahweh should be asked to validate a man's claim to membership of the community, and even of the priesthood, by recourse to the lottery of Urim and Thummim.

Ez 2:68. The lists are followed by yet another piece of parallelism with the exodus narrative. The people are asked to help in the furnishing of the new shrine, just as those at Sinai were enrolled to assist with the making of the shrine for the ark and the provision of vessels and vestments for the cult (Ex 25:2–7, 35:4–9).

Ez 2:70. The people live in scattered cities round Jerusalem because the capital is in ruins and can hardly provide shelter for those wretches who have been living there during the period when these comparatively prosperous Israelites were in Babylon. But evidently they all lived near enough to come into the city for the services conducted at the first altar among the rubble heaps.

At the end of this section we are confronted with a gathered community standing at the temple site in Jerusalem, a community of priests, levites, singers, gatekeepers, temple slaves, men of the city, men of the country farms. The Chronicler has presented us with 'all Israel' in little. The next section moves from the assembled congregation to the actual liturgy.

Ez 3:2–6. The priests set up the altar prescribed in the law of Moses on the old site selected by the angel of the plague when he appeared to David. This was obviously the holy place for all the inhabitants of Jerusalem and had been used by all sorts of folk for all kinds of ceremonies during the exilic absence of the official leaders of the cult. The men who return and claim the altar site for their own liturgical functions have reason to be nervous of those who had been using the site. But Yahweh is with them and they manage to hold the sacred site for themselves despite the grumblings of their neighbours.

The liturgy is suddenly in full swing. The offerings are burnt at the time of morning and evening prayer, and the people are said to be immediately settling into the liturgical cycle so that there are celebrations of the feast of tabernacles, the sabbaths, the new moon days and 'all the sacred festivals of Yahweh'. The impression given in the history is one of total cultic normality. The paragraph is beautifully designed, however, to bring the reader up short with a sudden halt at the last sentence of the cultic description: 'the temple of Yahweh was not yet reconstructed'.

1. What have we lost and gained by our modern weakening of family ties?

2. Do we have any faith in the use of lots to make decisions?

3. Does the liturgical year have much influence upon the way we think about the christian faith and its implementation?

Ez 3:7–4:24. Building the temple

The community now sets about the rebuilding of the temple. Everything comes together at this point: the edict of Cyrus made in a city so geographically and culturally distant from the men of Israel, the design of David and

Solomon in the long ago past, and the present need, all converge on the building of the temple.

The content and literary structure of this passage are based upon the description of the building of the first temple (though of course that description depended somewhat on the actual building of the second temple for its details: there is a reciprocity in such matters which is not easily elucidated). The stone-cutters, wood-carvers and carpenters are brought on again (cf 1 Chron 22:2 and 15), the wood again comes from Tyre and Sidon (cf 1 Chron 22:4 and 2 Chron 2:8 ff) and is paid for in the same way (cf 2 Chron 2:10). The laying of the foundation stone is again in the second month (cf 1 Kg 6:1, 2 Chron 3:2), and probably the foundation stones of the first temple were employed again since they must have remained at least roughly in place through all the upheavals and dilapidations of the superstructure (cf Ez 6:3).

The ritual trumpets sound again (cf 1 Chron 15:24), the cymbals clash again (cf 1 Chron 25:1 and 6) and, such is the devotion of the Chronicler to the old favourites, the same hymn is sung (cf 2 Chron 5:13 and 7:3). The Chronicler is not alone in his sentimental happiness at the world being itself again. Many of the people weep for the renewal of the liturgy in the temple.

Enter the villains. Wicked men attempt to prevent the reconstruction of the temple. Men who are unclean and have been forbidden to take part in the work and who are, therefore, frustrated and furious that the work should prosper. Those who are cast out of the liturgy react in the secular world with appropriate nastiness.

Having to account for the fact that the temple was not built up until the reign of Darius I, the Chronicler's view of the community did not allow him to blame, as Haggai and Zechariah blamed without remorse, the Israelites themselves for their lazy approach to the great task. The Chronicler blames the alien and the unclean. He transfers ritualistic categories to other areas so that their full effect may be appreciated by the reader. And henceforth avoided.

The shape of the Chronicler's view of the history of the temple up to the return from the exile comes out clearly in the reply of the Jerusalem leaders to the Persian governors:

(a) Yahweh long ago gave the people a temple
(b) Yahweh gave them also the pattern of liturgical service
(c) 'Our fathers irritated the God of the heavens' (the Chronicler does not use the name 'Yahweh' here because he wants to persuade the Persians that he was talking to them of things they could well understand, and the Persians referred to their chief deity as 'the God of the heavens')
(d) Yahweh gave them into the hands of the Babylonians (happily this could be regarded as a punishment by their hearers since the Persians thought of themselves as rescuing the world from the decadent Babylonians)
(e) Yahweh inspired Cyrus to order the rebuilding of the temple.

The history of the temple evidently fits quite perfectly that general pattern of Yahweh's dealings with Israel which was presented in the introduction to this commentary as the accustomed structure of Israelite historical explanation.

At this point we have been brought to the end of a section of the material. The Chronicler has traced events until they have arrived at the temple liturgy. The internal structure of the return has been described. The journey from Persia to Jerusalem has been presented as a manifestation of a movement from acknowledgement of sin to temple cult. The rest of Ezra–Nehemiah is a set of elaborations upon this theme developed from the story of two great men whom the Chronicler regarded as the heroes of the post-exilic renascence in Jerusalem.

1. How high among our requirements for a new town or housing estate would be the erection of a church?

2. Do we fully approve the rejection of the Samaritans by the orthodox at the rebuilding of Jerusalem?

Ez 5:1–6:22. A pause in the work

On the death of Cyrus reconstruction work in Jerusalem seems to have stopped, and it was not until Cambyses, his immediate successor, was also entombed with his ancestors, and Darius I had quieted the empire in a series of engagements with rebels in the west, that it seemed possible to return to the work. The emperor accepted the inheritance of Cyrus. He gave orders that the Jews should act upon the decree of the great king.

The state of the nation at the beginning of the reign of Darius I is described in the records of the prophet Haggai's speech to the governor and the high priest (Hag 1:1–11). Everywhere, the prophet says, he hears the people declare that the time is not yet ripe for the rebuilding of the temple.

Yahweh, however, has quite altered his mind from the time when David wanted to build a temple. Then Yahweh was content to live in a tent but now he is amazed that the men of Judah should be building houses for themselves and not thinking at all of a roof for Yahweh's house. The catastrophes that have afflicted the nation, the crop failures, the famine, the epidemics and the inflation, and perhaps even the bad weather, have all come upon the nation because there has been no attempt to make a hearth for Yahweh.

It is possible for us now to speculate whether it may not have been the people's being busy dealing with all their agricultural, health and economic troubles which kept them from having time to think about the temple, especially when the weather was so bad, but the prophet will not hear of such cart-before-the-horse explanations. Haggai's interpretation of such things is that they are punishments not causes.

After the interruption of the rebuilding by the Samaritan complaint, it took six months for Haggai to stir things enough to get the work begun again. The prophet knew that the people were discouraged by their memories of the first temple. The poor little temple that was being erected seemed worse than second-rate and made them all feel more keenly their present wretchedness. Haggai promised great things if only the people would purify their hearts and hands for the work (Hag 2:3–9).

Haggai's message was echoed by that of Zechariah. 'Return to me and I will return to you'. His dreams were imaginative leaps to a splendid future and are sometimes difficult to interpret but always there is a clear forward push in Zechariah's words to the time when Yahweh shall live among his own people in his own city. There will come a time when the men of the great nations will think it a happiness to make the golden journey to Jerusalem. They will crowd, jabbering in their many languages, to walk with a Jew to his city because, they will say, 'we have learnt that God is with you'.

Zechariah looks for a new messiah who will be the

prince of the Hebrew nation, riding like Solomon upon
a donkey as he comes into his capital Jerusalem, proclaiming peace to the world through his good favour to
the nations (Zech 9:9). And he looks too for a time (and
surely it must be soon) when the exiles will return from
Assyria and Egypt as at the exodus. 'The ban will be
lifted; Jerusalem will be safe to live in'. And the whole
race of men will come to celebrate the feast of tabernacles
at the Jerusalem sanctuary.

It is not part of my business to offer any detailed comment upon the work of these prophets, but it is evident
that an understanding of the kind of tasks imposed upon
the people and the kind of hopes they entertained at this
time is necessary for an appreciation of the Chronicler's
presentation of how those tasks were taken up and those
hopes fulfilled in the careers of Nehemiah, who built the
walls, and of Ezra, who celebrated the liturgy.

Though Haggai and Zechariah got the Jerusalem
people alert enough to their responsibilities so that they
again took up the matter of the temple under the
governorship of Zerubbabel, the descendant of David, the
work of reconstruction was nowhere near finished when
Nehemiah arrived in Jerusalem in 445. He had been
sent by Artaxerxes I to oversee the city. The nations of
the world have again found their place in the purpose of
Yahweh.

Nehemiah brought order to the city, and set things
going again despite the natural opposition of Sanballat,
the governor set by the Persians over Samaria, who had
at Nehemiah's coming lost a good section of his satrapy.
Later in Artaxerxes' reign Ezra came to put the temple
liturgy to rights.

The history of this period can be reconstructed in some
detail but more than the outline given here is not really
required to appreciate the general drift of the

Chronicler's interpretation of the history of the period of Nehemiah and Ezra. What is important for any reader of these books is the knowledge that, although the Chronicler had a number of useful historical sources at his command when he first made this history and is to be trusted in his treatment of most individual incidents, we do not now have his original text but one constructed out of the jumbled elements of his work. The order of individual sections in Ezra–Nehemiah has been shuffled so that the work has a sequence which the Chronicler would have found surprising. The later editor responsible for putting the sections in the order we now contemplate was, for example, either under the misapprehension that Ezra came before Nehemiah in the chronology of the events, or else supposed that because Ezra's work was more directly connected with the cult it should be placed before the more secular achievement of the wall-building layman, Nehemiah.

In these notes it will be assumed that the Chronicler's original order was in fact more in harmony with the chronology of events, not because the Chronicler cared more than his editor for the niceties of chronology, but because the order of events in history would seem happily to fit his religious reasons for setting out the events of the return.

Once the initial difficulty of jumping back and forth a little between Ezra and Nehemiah has been overcome, there will, I think, be the reward of a convincing sequence not unlike that originally intended by the Chronicler. It may be, of course, that a reader will prefer the later editor's version of the incident-order, as he finds it printed in a modern bible. If so, he will not find it arduous, I think, to find his way through these notes with the aid of the text. Anything that sends a reader back to the text is to be hallooed.

2

Nehemiah the governor
Neh 1:1–6:14; 12:1–13:30;
10:1–39

Neh 1:1–6:14. Building the walls

Neh 1:3. The site of Jerusalem is described as totally ruinous. It is as if there had never been a city there. Such is the tale brought to Nehemiah at Susa, the winter palace of the Persian kings.

Neh 1:5–11. Nehemiah's prayer is first of all a confession of the sins of the people. It is a corporate prayer designed by the Chronicler to place Nehemiah in our minds as the proper representative of Israel. And as a man who realises his representative character. The first person plural is used in the confession prayer.

The prayer puts the present sins into the perspective of the Mosaic covenant. The sins are breaches of the pledge of faith that the community has made to Yahweh. At the same time the prayer is the expression of a practical man's determination to persuade the Persian overlord to allow things to be put right. The combination of religious orthodoxy, community sense and practical acumen is a rare one and Nehemiah is obviously well fitted to be the hero of the reconstruction.

Nehemiah was the cup-bearer of Artaxerxes and therefore, since the cup-bearer served the queen as well as the king, a eunuch. A man of the Persian court, and a loyal

Jew, educated and faithful, Nehemiah was just the chap
to mediate between the men of Jerusalem and the great
king.

Neh 2:1–8. A serious man at all times, after months of
brooding on the affairs of his people and their holy city
he must have been particularly gloomy looking and quite
out of place at the feasting. Remarks about the graves of
Nehemiah's fathers must have seemed not at all the sort
of thing for a banquet. The party would not survive
many of those. No wonder Artaxerxes made an effort
to cheer him up. And no wonder he gave way to the cup-
bearer's plea to do something about the state of the ancestral cemetery.

Nehemiah, like David and Solomon, begins his business by setting about the provision of timber for the
building (cf 1 Kg 5; 2 Chron 2 : 8 ff).

Neh 2:10. The opponents of Nehemiah named here are
officials of the Persian king and represent the two kinds
of enemy with which Yahwism had always had to con-
tend. Sanballat was a Samaritan of mixed blood, a worshipper of the Canaanite god Horon, and Tobiah, the
governor of Ammon, though certainly a Yahwist, was
not above a little syncretism now and then, and had later
to be expelled from the temple precincts (Neh 13 : 4 ff).

Neh 2:11–20. After three days Nehemiah rises in the
night to begin the work of renewal. This is a literary pre-
echo that might well be introduced when men are discussing the significance of the details of the resurrection
prophecies and narratives in the gospels.

He tours the city walls and sees how it is that Jerusalem is thought to be a nothing on the political map.
His morning speech to the people is based upon religious

motives but the citizens would be quick to appreciate the political advantages of living within a walled city of some strength. If the walls were built up they would appear to the world as the favoured friends of the Persian king.

The reply of Nehemiah to the accusations of the three provincial governors is both politically astute in its Persian phrasing of devotion to 'the god of the heavens', and religiously pure in its refusal to allow any syncretist nonsense in the new Jerusalem.

Neh 3:1-32. In chapter three it is apparent that the Chronicler wants to make clear to his readers that 'all Israel' was eager to take a share in the rebuilding of the city. Here we seem to be reading material taken by the Chronicler from a source in the temple archives. Perhaps he had looked over a list of the building foremen.

Obviously Nehemiah had planned the enterprise very carefully. The sections of wall are not of equal length but are adapted to the resources of the rebuilder tribe or family. The Chronicler is perhaps more interested in showing what a common effort the work was than to give any details of the work itself. He records the participation of Eliashib, the high priest and his fellow priests, 3:1, the levites, 3:17, the gate-keepers, 3:29, the guilds, 3:31, and the various groups of laymen.

Neh 3:33-4:23. A certain fierceness comes into the story just at this point. From 3:33 to 4:17 the opposition becomes keener. Personal fun is made of the men on the walls, 3:33-35, and Nehemiah's prayer to Yahweh is designed quite deliberately to encourage Yahweh to take a heavy revenge upon the mockers. Then from insult the enemies turn to threats. Nehemiah answers these with an appeal to Yahweh's protective power, and a practical step of dividing his forces between building and spear-carrying. The unskilled workers went armed about their business now.

That not every Jew was confident that Nehemiah would bring off his plan is shewn by the popular song preserved at 4:4. And that not everyone was convinced that the covenant was all that effective an instrument in the setting up of a good society, becomes clear when the tales told by Jews about other Jews are placed before the reader. Many of those working on the walls must have been sceptical about the promise of a new society because they could not have had all that much confidence in the good will of their fellow Jews.

Neh 5:1–11. The womenfolk urge the men to complain about the state of Israelite society. Their complaints bring into the open the appalling Jewish traffic in slave Jews. To buy enough food and to pay the Persian taxes, the poor found themselves forced to give up to other Jews first their rights over their strips of land, and then their children as pledges to money-lenders. In such a situation the rich get richer and the poor poorer. The slaves have a continuously diminishing chance of ever being redeemed.

The money-lenders seem to have belonged to those groups who had married foreigners. They had certainly made a deal of money out of the Persian occupation of their country and the wretchedness of their fellows in the covenant community.

Nehemiah's authority was put to full stretch in his dealing with this horrifying threat to his community and its reconstruction of the city. He berated those Jewish officials and leaders who took as pledges men who had already been redeemed from foreign bondage. And they, quite naturally, took no notice of this religious maniac who was interfering with their property and profit. Like Lord Melbourne these political leaders thought it outrageous that religion should interfere with a man's private life.

Neh 5:12–19. The leaders remaining obdurate, Nehemiah called an assembly of the people. The oppressed, of course, voted hugely against the oppressors, and Nehemiah (remembering perhaps the slave owners of Jer 34:8 ff) bound the merchants, money-lenders and political quislings with an oath and a curse that they should release at once their poor captives.

Nehemiah was in a strong position in this matter. The people knew that although the Persian king had authorised Nehemiah to levy a tax on the men of Judah to support his government, Nehemiah had not taxed his people. He and his brothers had not only paid for the support of their official staff but had redeemed destitute Jews from their slavery out of their private purses. That this expenditure was huge is indicated by the number of men Nehemiah housed and fed in his official residence.

The Chronicler's description of Nehemiah leads the reader to appreciate this governor as a greatly good man. The attempts of the Persian officials to dispose of him appear, therefore, as particularly despicable pieces of political jobbery.

The governors' plot is too bald a piece of wickedness to trap a man of Nehemiah's good sense; the suggestion that he will be accused to the Persian king of conspiring to make himself an independent ruler with messianic pretensions is dismissed by Nehemiah as an effective lie; the prophecy of Shemaiah, the quisling seer, designed to entice Nehemiah into breaking the law (for a layman and a eunuch had no right to enter the temple) declares itself by its content to be a false saying and Nehemiah

has no truck with such palterings; the diplomatic activity
of Tobiah and his relations among the Persian provincial
officials comes to nothing. Nehemiah is not to be frighted
by such things. The wall is completed.

*1. Once we come to deal with Babylonians and Per-
sians do we feel more confident in the historical re-
liability of the narrative than we do when we are reading
only of the Hebrews and their temple?*

*2. What has produced the present situation in which
christians seems to want a more personally-involving
faith than before, and to want less those public aspects
that Lord Melbourne thought the only proper ones?*

Neh 12:1–13:30. Purification

Nehemiah began his ordering of the city's life by re-
establishing the old covenant responses in a form appropriate to the new conditions. Men were appointed to
take charge of the temple finances, and the Chronicler
is pleased to add that every one was very happy to con-
tribute to the upkeep of the temple and the payment of
the sacred ministers.

When, however, Nehemiah went back to serve his
turn again in the Persian court the people stopped sending in their tithes to support the levites, and the levites,
not caring for this new life of poverty, gave up their
temple ministry and went back to farming. Nehemiah
had to bring them all back to the temple and secure their
salaries before the liturgy could be re-started (cf 13:10–
13).

Foreigners were told to go far off from the cultic
centre, and to take their religions with them. That this
was a matter of some delicacy and importance is shewn

by Neh 13, where the high priest Eliashib is said to have
provided lodgings in the temple complex itself for his
syncretist relation Tobiah, who had already caused a
great deal of trouble to the Chronicler's hero. The high
priest could only have dared have such a guest in the
temple if Nehemiah were away in Persia. When Nehemiah returned with permission from the king for another
long stay in Jerusalem the intruding Tobiah was hurried
out of the place. A ceremonial cleansing of the room in
which Tobiah had lodged must have impressed the
people of Jerusalem with Nehemiah's zeal for Yahweh's
law, for Tobiah was a great official and not without influence in Persia, and he could not have relished the intelligence that Nehemiah had had his room purified.

Neh 13:15–31. Further, Nehemiah restored the full observance of the sabbath and stopped the market trading
that the Samaritan country folk had begun to conduct in
Jerusalem on that day. The Jewish farmers had come
to the markets too in order not to lose profit through
zeal. The farmers were not at all anxious to give up their
market day and squatted several sabbaths in front of the
gates of Jerusalem that Nehemiah had closed against
them. He had to threaten to use the soldiery against
them before they would go away. And, perhaps fearing
that the soldiers might well start trading themselves with
the farmers if they were left to themselves on the gates,
Nehemiah placed the levitical guard from the temple at
the gate. The levites could serve as guards on the sabbath because Nehemiah counted it a holy work to pre-
serve the holy rest.

The quietude and solemnity of the cult was
threatened, too, by the marriages that many Jews had
contracted with foreign girls, like the mixed-blood Samaritans or the pagan Moabites. The careful exclusion of

the Ammonite and Moabite persons from marriage with the Jews is insisted upon by the Chronicler because of the legislation of Deut 23 : 3. The children of marriages with pagans could not speak Hebrew and Nehemiah was very anxious to revive the holy language as the spoken word of the holy people. This would work mightily for the maintenance of cultic purity and racial identity. That Nehemiah's authority was tremendous in the community may be gauged by his exiling the grandson of the high priest for entering into a marriage with one of the treacherous Sanballat family.

Neh 10:1–39. The laws of Nehemiah

The difficulties faced by Nehemiah are precisely those dealt with in the code of Neh 10, and it would seem that these regulations were ordained by Nehemiah after his return from the court at Babylon and his discovery of the lax way in which the community was interpreting their responsibilities as members of the covenant. They were as follows:

  (i) Marriage with foreign men and women is forbidden to all who would take a share in the life of Jerusalem
 (ii) The sabbath rest from trading must be observed by all whether between Jew and Gentile or Jew and Jew
(iii) The seventh year release from debts must be fully honoured between Jew and Jew
 (iv) The tithes for the support of the temple and levites must be paid regularly
  (v) The cultic duties of the people, including the provision of wood for the sacrificial pyres and attendance in person at the feast, must be observed.

It is to be noted that Nehemiah is only attempting to deal with the future in these regulations. He does not, for instance, make any effort to persuade the Jews to divorce the Gentiles they have already married. That sort of retrospective legislation was not introduced until the community was much more settled within Jewish law.

We are presented here with the community's response to Nehemiah's moderate reform. The living out of a demanding renewal of their society had not yet been tried and the men did not perhaps understand how much was being demanded of them.

1. Are there any rituals of purification in our society? Do we even 'spring-clean' any more?

2. What significance has the transferred holiness of Sunday in our society? Do we approve the thinking behind the sabbath rest?

3. What are we to think of Nehemiah's condemnation of marriage between persons of mixed race?

3
The assembly
Neh 6:15–7:73; 11:1–36;
Ez 7:1–10:44; Neh 9:1–38;
8:1–18

Neh 6:15–7:73. Starting afresh

At the completion of the wall life can be ordered properly within the city. Nehemiah sets about making the civic life a pattern of harmonious co-operation. He sets guards at the gates (the Chronicler puts his favourites the levites at this post because he wants to suggest that none other was trustworthy, but this seems an unconvincing elaboration of the command) and Nehemiah is careful to put them under commanders he can rely on to support his authority.

Twilight and dawning are the times of surprise attacks, so the gates are opened only at full light and each district is ordered to provide its borough militia for its own defence.

Having built the town and made it secure, Nehemiah sets to work encouraging new men to come and live in the city and make their homes there rather than settle in the country districts. He has lists made of those who have recently settled in their ancestral towns, and hopes that men will be confident enough in his promise of security to bring their families into Jerusalem itself.

Neh 11:1–36. Populating the city

The lack of men to populate Jerusalem was overcome by the search for volunteers and, when these failed to amount to enough, the drawing of lots among the farmdwellers and provincial townsmen. The Chronicler was pleased enough with those who came to list the settlers as public benefactors. And he must be reflecting Nehemiah's own delight with these men, since the list is evidently derived from Nehemiah's records. But there were still not enough inhabitants for the city to feel that it was going to have a good future.

It may be that when Nehemiah went back to the Persian court he drummed up support for a second set of Jews to return to Jerusalem from their Babylonish homes. The present version of Ezra–Nehemiah suggests that Ezra came to the city before Nehemiah but it may well be that Ezra was persuaded by Nehemiah's efforts to build up both walls and population for Jerusalem to become himself a member of the city community.

Ez 7:1–10:44. The new liturgy

At any rate the Chronicler moves now from talking of the building of the city and the sanctuary to describing an assembly of the people for the liturgy. Nehemiah certainly could not have been responsible for this part of the renewal. The despised status of the eunuch in Israel at this period is to be discerned in Is 56:3–5 where the foreigner and the eunuch are lumped together and promised that although they now are outcasts from the central action of the covenant they will, if they observe the law, have a part in the coming era of the kingdom. The passage takes it for granted that the eunuch has at this time no part at all in the temple services.

It is interesting to observe that Isaiah's promise, if it could not be realised in the life-time of the good Nehemiah, was brought to event when Philip the disobedient deacon paid no attention to the customs of his apostolic superiors and baptised the eunuch minister of the Kandake of Ethiopia, and thus invented the universal community of the church.

(i) Ez 7:1–8:20. Ezra assembles the folk

Ezra has an unimpeachable family record and is highly skilled in the interpretation of the law of Moses. Surrounded by the priests, the levites, the singers, the gate-keepers and the temple servants he is the epitome of ecclesiastical orthodoxy.

The Persian king is inspired by Yahweh to encourage an assembling of the men of Israel, and his empowering of Ezra to be his representative is understood by the Chronicler as the necessary human means for Ezra's being designated the leader of Israel. The coming together of foreign civil power and Yahweh's will brings about a properly shaped history. The event is put into literary structure by the rounding off of the account of Artaxerxes' decree by a liturgical doxology.

The list of families is the fulfilment of the demand for a congregation; laymen, priests, and the specially emphasised levitical complement, are assembled for the pilgrimage journey to go up to Jerusalem.

(ii) Ez 8:21–3. The confessional service

Knowing that sin prevents any enterprise coming to success those who, like the exodus folk or those who shared in the pilgrim caravans of Solomon's time, mean to 'go up to Jerusalem' inquire for the 'right way'—which has a moral as well as a geographical significance—so that they shall not forsake the way of the Lord. After the journey the pilgrims complete this part of their service with an examination of conscience for the whole people.

Ezra stands at the centre of the congregation and speaks the confession for all the sins of the people who have forsaken the integrity of the holy race. Foreign marriages are uppermost in his mind. Racial purity is important for the renewal of a city which is to be peculiarly Jewish.

Ezra's demonstration of repentance in pulling out his hair, tearing his clothes and sitting desolate before the temple, is certainly a continuance of Jeremiah's prophetic mimes, but it is also a realisation of the actual state of the people: his prayer moves from a personal comment on the others, 'I am profoundly ashamed . . .', to an acknowledgement on behalf of all, 'We have remained in great guilt . . .'.

The confession is followed by an act of corporate repentance. All the people wept profusely and declared their intention of returning to the covenant and putting away their foreign wives.

The cleansing of the family is recorded in some detail so that there is a permanent record of the renewal of the purity of the individual family and the whole nation.

1. Do we now believe that there is but one 'way of the Lord'? How far are morals to be regarded as relative to times and places?

2. What is the purpose and effectiveness of a private confession of sin? Why do some find that public penance services give greater help in the service of Christ?

Some textual matters

Since Neh 9 and a great deal of the next four chapters in that book are patently out of sequence, for it is manifestly improbable that a day of penance should follow immediately upon that feast of tabernacles described in Neh 8, these obtrusive chapters have to be found another home. Since they fit perfectly as the conclusion of the penitential chapters at the end of Ezra it would seem proper to deal with them here.

The obvious place for the Neh 9 penance service is after the expulsion of the foreign wives. This is in fact supported by Neh 9:2 where it is declared that those who had had relations with the foreigners stood up and confessed their sin against the law.

(iii) Neh 9:1–38. The penitential prayer

The prayer begins with the praise of Yahweh as creator, and continues with the history of Yahweh's grace to his own people at the covenant with Abraham, the exodus redemption and the giving of the law. The declarations here of power and love are followed by references to the sin of the people in chasing after false gods who have no power and no love for the folk. This is then high-lighted as an offence by further declarations of Yahweh's steadfast loyalty in bringing such a sinful people to possession of the land of Canaan.

From the primitive history of the people before they crossed into Canaan the praise passes to contemplation of the history of the kingdoms of Israel and Judah, the military ups and downs, the waverings of the people, and the continual compassion of Yahweh for the people through their experience of defeat, exile and return. On the basis of this evidence of Yahweh's grace the prayer moves into a confident cry for Yahweh's love to be with the people in the present situation.

The whole section is characterised by the Chronicler's confidence in prayer as the power which will deal with history. Yahweh will forgive the man who humbles himself and forgiveness will be followed by the gracious sign of prosperity.

(iv) Neh 8:1–12. The reading of the law

The assembly is now confronted with its responsibilities as the covenant people. The law is read by Ezra to the people as they stand in reverence to the word of Yahweh (cf the christian congregation's habit of standing for the gospel reading).

Ezra begins with the blessing customarily used at the beginning of readings from the word of Yahweh during the Chronicler's lifetime, and the people respond with the ritual response. He reads in Hebrew and the levites translate the passages into popular Aramaic. The scene is wholly ecclesiastic in its arrangement and the Chronicler evidently thinks of this renewal of the assembly at the reading of the law as the final necessary preparation for the celebration of the liturgy. In the morning the proclamation is made that the law commands the celebration of 'the feast'. Everything is right again.

(v) Neh 8:13–18. The feast

Tabernacles is *the* feast (cf, for example, 1 Kg 8:2, and 65, Josephus *Antiquities* VIII, iv, 1 and Jn 7). The origins of the celebration are to be found in a farmers' thanksgiving for the harvest (Ex 23:16, Deut 16:13) and a great deal was eaten and drunk during the days of the celebration (cf 1 Sam 1:14 f). After the huge meals the pilgrims joined in wild dances of an erotic character through the lanes of the vineyards (cf Jg 21:19–21). Even in new testament times barriers had to be set up during these dances in Jerusalem to keep the men and women apart (cf my *Community Witness*, London 1967, pp 127–48).

The regulations about the booths made from branches set down in Neh 8.13–18 depend a great deal upon Lev 23, especially verses 42–43 (Lev 23: 40–41 belong to a period later than the Chronicler so he could not employ them in his account of the festival in the first autumn of Ezra's high priesthood).

Plutarch (*Quaest conv* iv, 6) quite properly saw a likeness between the feast of tabernacles and the Bacchus cult he had watched in various towns of the empire. Certainly since the feast was not celebrated by the Israelites until they came into Canaan there must be a presumption of some pagan origin (cf Jg 21:19–21 for a reference to the festival kept by the men of Shechem in honour of their pagan god at the time when the Israelites were dancing for Yahweh).

The hutments made out of branches in which the Hebrews lived for the days of the feast are probably derived from those huts of branches made in the vineyards to shelter the harvesters. They are certainly not derived from the tents of the exodus journey, though later Jews tried to establish this interpretation as being properly pious.

The celebration of the feast is therefore a sign both of economic stability—the harvest is gathered, there will be food and drink for the coming year—the settled state of the civil government—it is possible to relax and not worry about the enmities of Samaritans for a while—and the cosmological harmony—all is right with a world in

which the people of Yahweh can come singing to meet
his love in Jerusalem.

It was on such a note of restored happiness that the
Chronicler could end his account of the history of Israel.

*1. Like Wagner, the Chronicler thought that con-
tinual recapitulation of 'the story so far' was necessary
for the significance of events to be grasped by his reader.
How far is this true of us?*

*2. How can city-dwellers enter into the country-
man's concern with the agricultural cycle that is assumed
in these writings? Is the liturgical cycle equally difficult
to make meaningful for ourselves in the continuous on-
rush of town life?*

1 Maccabees

Introduction

Maccabeus seems to be derived from *maqqabah*, a hammer. Judas Maccabeus is like 'the hammer of the Scots' as he flattens all opposition in the Levant. That the title was a flattering one which everybody wanted for himself can be discerned from the progressive widening of its application from Judas, the third son of the priest Mattathias, to his whole family and their descendants in the Hasmonaean royal family, and then to the unrelated group of a mother and her seven sons in 2 Maccabees 7.

Originally 1 Maccabees was called *The book of the house of the princes of God*. It was composed by a Palestinian Jew who much admired the Hasmonaean house. His first draft of the history has passed through several editorial hands, the last of which added the final three chapters, and translated the Hebrew original into Greek.

Having called the shaper of Samuel and Kings 'the Deuteronomist', the editor of Judges 'the historian' and, quite uninventively, the maker of Chronicles 'the Chronicler', our present author may be termed 'the writer', and the author of 2 Maccabees as we have it may be distinguished as 'the epitomist', since he gives a condensed version of the five books of Jason of Cyrene (2 Mac 2 : 19–23).

After a prologue concerned with the predecessors of

the main characters, with Alexander the Great and the
priest Mattathias, the writer tells the story of three Jewish leaders: Judas, who fought for the religious liberty
of his people (3 : 1–9 : 22), Jonathan, who extended their
territorial possessions far out from Jerusalem (9 : 23–
12 : 53), and Simon, who gave them political independence (13 : 1–16 : 17), and the history is brought to a close
with the accession of John Hyrcanus I (16 : 18–24).

The writer certainly worked from the established records of his folk, like the temple chronicles that he
refers to at 16 : 23, and the diplomatic archives of the
Hasmonaean family, which included the exchanges he
cites between the princes and the Roman senate, and
most probably he had access to eye-witness accounts of
some of the later incidents. Perhaps, indeed, he was himself present at some of the events. He seems to have been
a careful and conscientious narrator, providing the
reader with a vast amount of material to supplement
what he may find in the accounts of Polybius, Livy and
Appian.

The writer does not seem to have put much trust in
princes, Syrian, Egyptian or Jewish, and none at all in
oligarchies like the Spartan magistrates or the Roman
senate. His whole trust was in the law (1 : 56 f) and the
prophets (9 : 54), and he made it clear that even Simon,
the greatest of the Hasmonaean princes, was merely
holding the fort until Yahweh should establish his own
rule openly among his people. The psalm of wonder
(14 : 4–15) is made from a selection of scriptural passages
descriptive of the golden age which, while allowing
Simon's virtue to have full praise, take the reader back
to the source of glory and give him a new urgency in his
prayers for the reign of Yahweh.

There is always a tension in the writer's mind between

his desire to bring his readers back to an appreciation of the covenant under which they will have life abundantly, and his recognition that the new elements of sophistication in his society make it improbable that his words will be given much attention. The tension is particularly noticeable in the writer's accounts of the battles against the Syrian forces. He wants his people to understand that these battles are the most recent incidents in the old holy war, but he sees that they are conducted not by prayer and fasting but by political and tactical skills. The accounts of the battles are lumpy pieces of literature because the writer cannot bring himself to surrender the true pattern of the holy war when he is composing his account of the fight, and yet cannot abandon his loyalty to the facts which must be set down even though they do not fit the pattern.

A further indication in the writing that he was unwilling to accept the new ideas which were altering the balances of the old covenant faith can be seen in his omission of any reference to a life after death. The writer belongs with the wealthier Sadducean party rather than with the modernist Pharisees who comforted their poorer followers with talk of rewards in another world for all that they suffer here. The writer is evidently the last of the good conservatives.

1

Mattathias
1 Mac 1:1–2:70

1 Mac 1:1–10. Background

Alexander the Great was, by the time our man came to
write his account of the Maccabean period in the Levant,
a distant and hazy figure. Alexander's generals, like
those of Napoleon, managed to secure for themselves
through the very break-up of the empire a number of
little kingdoms of which the most powerful were Mace-
donia, Syria and Egypt. Palestine, as usual, was caught
up in the power rivalries of her neighbours. Ptolemy
Lagi grabbed Palestine at the original division of Alexander's territories but lost it in 315 to Antigonus of
Syria, regaining the area at Gaza in 312, withdrawing
again the next year, but reoccupying the territory after
the defeat of Antigonus at Ipsus in 301. And so it went
on.

During the years of crisis, 202–198, most Jews in Palestine were hopeful that Antiochus the Great of Syria
would gain control of the country, and these carried the
others at the Council of Elders, so that when, at the battle
of Panion in 198, Antiochus the Great finally established
himself in command of Palestine, he rewarded the Jews
by giving orders for the restoration of the war-damaged
temple, exempted the cult officials from taxes for three
years, ordered the restitution of property to those who

lost their possessions in the wars, decreed death for the gentiles who dared enter the temple, and prohibited the introduction of unclean animals to Jerusalem.

In Egypt a great number of the Jews had settled down comfortably and established a synagogue in Alexandria which undertook to provide a Greek translation of the scriptures for those Jews who had become so much a part of the gentile world that they could not read the old Hebrew. This Septuagint version became important as providing an entry into Jewish culture for the Greek-speaking peoples of the Roman empire.

It was evident that the Syrians and Egyptians were both making efforts to establish themselves as the proper protectors of the Jews and the proper landlords of Palestine. It was evident to the Jews who waited for another war. It was evident to the Romans who determined that there should be a balance of power in the area which would preclude war. The Roman diplomats failed to prevent Antiochus marching into Egypt in 190 so the Senate sent in an army which ruinously defeated Antiochus the Great at Magnesia. The Syrian had to hand over his own son, Antiochus Epiphanes, as a hostage to Rome and his treasury was emptied by the exactions of the victors. The poor man lived on in misery for three years and was succeeded in 187 by his eldest son Seleucus IV. The Romans sensed that their hold on Syria would be greater if they had a hostage nearer in blood to the new king, so Seleucus' son, Demetrius, took Antiochus' place in Rome and the prince went off to Athens where the people received him kindly and made him chief magistrate.

On the murder of Seleucus IV by his minister Heliodorus, Antiochus Epiphanes rushed to Antioch, ousted the usurper and, excluding the hostage Demetrius, made himself king.

Antiochus Epiphanes had to deal quickly with three huge problems, his lack of funds, the rivalries of various groups within his empire, and the pressures of foreign powers. He never got himself free of foreign threats but he restored his finances by confiscating the treasures from the shrines of the various cults in the empire including, of course, those of the Jerusalem temple. He decided to obliterate the cultural bases of faction in his empire by enforcing Greek notions, which he had learnt in Athens, on all his subjects. He found hellenising friends everywhere, including the city of Jerusalem. These hellenists in the absence of the pro-Egyptian high priest, Onias III, obtained the elevation of his hellenist brother Jason. This high priest was so delighted with gentile manners that he never employed the Hebrew form of his name, Joshua, and he entered eagerly into the hellenisation of the city's life. A gymnasium was built, games organised, and the young men of better family turned to Greek ways —they had their circumcision mark disguised so that they might run naked without provoking derisive gentile comment, they wore the cap of Hermes, patron of athletes, adopted all manner of Greek practices and, according at least to Fr Corbishley in the *New Catholic Commentary* on these events, 'the Greeks were notoriously given to unnatural vice'.

Orthodox Jews, famous and natural in every way, disliked all this of course, but worse was to come. Jason was deposed by the great men of the city because he was not hellenist enough and a new man, Menelaus, who was not even a member of the high priestly family, was installed by the Syrian military amid civil commotion. The new man found that the treasury was empty and he could not fulfil his promise of monies for the Syrians. He was summoned to Antioch to explain how it was that he could not pay the proper price for being made high priest and there was confronted by the infuriated Onias III who was still living in hope of returning to Jerusalem. Menelaus made friends with Antiochus' minister, Andronicus, who had Onias executed. Menelaus just managed to raise the necessary bribe for this and felt much more secure.

It may be that Onias III, the last Zadokite high priest, is the 'Teacher of Righteousness' and Menelaus the 'Wicked Priest' of Qumran mythology.

  1. What are we now to think, in our desire to give due honour to all human achievements, of the Jewish rejection of the Greek culture?

  2. How far ought we to go in our recognition of value in 'humanism', 'communism' and 'atheism'? When does dialogue stop?

1 Mac 1:11–2:28. Antiochus and the Jewish reaction

Antiochus outraged orthodox Hebrew opinion in 169 by a proclamation that he was to be addressed as *Theos Epiphanes*, 'God manifest', and again in 166 when he claimed the equally divine title *Nicephorus*, 'Victorious'. What outraged the Jews disturbed the Romans. Antiochus Epiphanes was constrained to sign a treaty with the senate which included a clause promising non-aggression in the Levant and, on his breaking the treaty and invading Egypt, Antiochus found himself unceremoniously ordered to leave the country. He went slinking back to Syria in an ugly mood and, hearing at this moment of disturbances in Jerusalem, he sent the Mysian mercenaries to quieten the place.

The walls of Jerusalem were cast down, women forced

into slavery as army camp servants, and a permanent Greek citadel, the Akra, established opposite the temple to prevent any further trouble. The rule of the city was given to an army commander and he gave some semblance of authority to the hellenising priests who imposed heavy taxes on their orthodox countrymen and watched unconcernedly as the temple was taken over by the mercenaries for their own cults. The worship of Yahweh was absorbed in the rituals of Baal Shamen. At this point the writer takes up his account of the history of the Maccabean revolt.

1 Mac 1:23. The writer is much concerned with ritual instruments, the lamp-stand, the thurible, and the libation-cup. These he can list with some emotion. It does not seem that he could discover much first-hand evidence of popular lamentation for the filching of these things. He had to resort to what some commentators call 'high poetry', but which seems to be rather empty rhetoric about young men wasting away, brides sitting disconsolate on their honey-moon night, and earthquakes rattling the wine cups.

1 Mac 1:31. The sack of Jerusalem in 586 had been an experience so terrible that in new testament times the Jews had used imagery from that catastrophe to describe the last days. The account had come to have universal significance. But the description of the Mysian general's occupation of the city cannot be worked up, however hard the writer tries, to something as emotionally stirring.

1 Mac 1:41. Active repression of the Jewish cult was an element of Antiochus' policy of achieving some cultural uniformity in his territory. Sanctuary libations, sabbath rests, and circumcisions are proscribed and many Israelites, as the writer is forced to admit, seem not to care a jot for their loss, and are joining in pagan dances and running naked in the sports arenas.

1 Mac 1:57. The climax of the wickedness comes when Antiochus erects his pagan altar on top of the Yahwist stepped altar in the temple. By imposing a small slab Antiochus turned the old altar stone into the last step up to the new.

1 Mac 1:62. On the other hand, despite the systematic eradication of orthodox obedience to the law, a number of Jews remained faithful to the old way of life. These conservatives were less molested in the country towns than at the Jerusalem centre of government, and Mattathias at first seems to have thought that he could live the good life in Modein, but the inspections of the farmsteads for copies of the law and signs of orthodox faith forced the priest and his sons to make an open choice.

1 Mac 2:8. It is difficult to sympathise with so materialist and clerical a man, for few of us now can care much about a building and fewer still can believe that any nation's vitality can be so bound up with maces and cups that 'the vessels were her glory'. But Mattathias deserves our admiration in his stand for his belief against the blandishments and threats offered by the royal officers.

He must have been an imposing character, for the men seem to have simply stood by watching while Mattathias wrestled with the quisling and the government agent. The writer sees in Mattathias a priest who will bring about a renewal of the old life. Mattathias is like the redoubtable Phenehas who once righteously thrust a spear right through an Israelite and his Midianite girl when he caught them in an alcove (cf Num 25:8). The writer delights in his picture of violent clerics heading nationalist crowds. The call is for a return 'to the covenant' and it sounds fine, but the reader should beware of relinquishing his hold on reality here. Mattathias' loyalty to the covenant is not to be disentangled from a concern with the accidental oddities the writer has been lamenting.

1. Does the distinction between rural conservatism and urban radicalism persist despite the effects of mass media?

2. What part does the ritual and its vessels play in the retention of religious loyalties of modern christians?

1 Mac 2:29–70. Victory and death

The people of the covenant congregate in the desert and the rebellion achieves an exodus dignity. The procession of men, women, children and cattle into the desert is pursued by the foreign oppressor. But the likeness to the exodus is not taken all the way. Yahweh does not intervene. The men of the law obey the sabbath restriction on all activity and stand to be slaughtered by the Syrian army.

1 Mac 2:39. Mattathias is more realist than they, and he abrogates the sabbath regulation in order to make way for self-defence. This may be the beginning of that process of accepting the world's standards which later Hasmonaeans perfected in their luxurious Jerusalem palaces.

1 Mac 2:45. At any rate Mattathias and his men take it as proper that he who has the power should dictate the forms of life for the people. Virtue is enforced by military means. A man may kill sinners with a sense of his good deed for the day being accomplished. Further

rituals are demanded from the people and boys are forcibly circumcised.

It may be that we do not appreciate the importance of
such rites for Mattathias and his folk, and so feel hesitant
to judge what is going on. But there is no demand upon
us to approve the deed as well as the intention in Mattathias' reformation. We are not to surrender the sophistication of our judgement simply in order to approve the
primitive.

1 Mac 2:51. The dying Mattathias is given a speech
which puts his rebellion in proper line with the old wars
of holiness against wicked heathendom. The priest belongs with the patriarchs, the judges, the kings and the
prophets.

1 Mac 2:61. Mattathias offers a promise of vindication
in this life and a reminder that no man lasts for ever.
The doctrine of a life beyond death is not yet part of the
writer's orthodoxy. Like David, Mattathias demands vengeance on the enemy; the pagans are to be paid back in
full.

*1. Is there in our own national culture any past event
with anything like the mythological power of the exodus
in Jewish life?*

*2. What influence does the doctrine of a life after
death have on our present actions?*

2

Judas
1 Mac 3:1–9:22

1 Mac 3:1–4:61. Holy war and temple dedication

1 Mac 3:3–9. These verses may be derived from a popular song of the period, or even may be patterned on a sophisticated acrostic upon *Judas Maccabeus*; certainly, like other passages of 1 Maccabees, they betray their Hebrew original.

1 Mac 3:12. The sword of the Syrian general in the hand of Judas was a constant reminder of this early success over the pagan. The story of this significant sword carries echoes of the tale of David bearing to his battles the captured sword of the Philistine Goliath (cf 1 Sam 21 : 9).

1 Mac 3:13. This episode has all the makings of a holy war. The flamboyant hopes of the commander of the huge pagan force and the fear of the small Israelite force ought, on the old pattern, to lead into a wondrous account of Yahweh's victory. But the days of the holy war, like those of the exodus, are not easily recaptured.

Yahweh did not intervene at the sabbath slaying of the thousand (1 Mac 2.39 ff) and he is not asked to win this battle for his people. The purely human motives characteristic of any little nationalist army are alleged: 'we are fighting for our lives and our laws'. It may be that an appeal to Yahweh is concealed from us by shy references to *heaven* (3:18 and 19) and the personal affirmation to which they lead: 'he will crush them'. But the victory is described not in terms of prayer and ritual trumpeting, but in terms of military dash which brought a warrior's fame to Judas in every nation.

1 Mac 3:41. The writer has so exaggerated the importance of events in this small province of the Syrian empire that it is useful to be reminded of the smallness of the Jewish army by the description of the vulturesque Edom merchants coming to buy the Israelite captives of the morrow's battle.

This detail is well-placed by the writer. It has the same effect in the narrative as the description in *Henry V* of the French princes playing at dice for the English before Agincourt.

1 Mac 3:46. After the desecration of the temple in 167 orthodox Jews had built a substitute shrine at Mizpah to the north of Jerusalem. Sacrifices were not offered there, for the law demanded that this element of the cult be centralised at Jerusalem, but the orthodox met at Mizpah for prayer, the reading of the law, and the collection of tithes.

Mizpah was associated with Samuel (cf 1 Sam 7:5 f), but Judas had none of the old seer's immediate knowledge of Yahweh's will. The old method of trusting to Yahweh's control through the chances of Urim and Thummin, is now employed for the reading of the scriptures. Like any other fundamentalist, Judas obeys the cry *tolle, lege,* and opens the law at random in the expectation of receiving Yahweh's guidance. Even our writer has a moment of unease when he admits that this procedure is like that of pagans approaching their gods at the oracle shrines. However, prayer and trumpetings

make the ceremony more conformable to the old pattern
of things and it seems acceptable.

1 Mac 3:55. The men are arranged in companies for the
holy enterprise. It is interesting that Jesus is said to have
arranged the men in like companies before the feeding
of the five thousand (cf Mk 6:39–40).

1 Mac 3:56. Of greater interest is the admission here
of precisely those excuses which the king of Jesus' parable
did not allow to justify a man's not coming to his feast
(cf Lk 14:18–19). The dismissal of some part of the
force is not, like that of Gideon, done at the instigation
of Yahweh in order to demonstrate the divine origin of
the coming victory. Judas is quite ready to admit that his
men may well all die next day.

1 Mac 4:1. The battle with the main Syrian force under
Nicanor and the skirmish with Gorgias' patrol ends with
total Jewish victory. And the men celebrate, as they
gather up their share of the booty, by singing the trium-
phal Psalm 118. This event gets as near to a holy war as
any in the narrative. It begins with a reference to the
exodus (4:9), continues with trumpet calls (4:12) and
sudden panics (4:21), and ends with a cultic psalm
(4:24).

But the next encounter is wholly like ordinary fights
between those who believe God to be on their side. The
prayer to Yahweh (4:30–33) leads not to a wondrous act
of divine love and power, but to soldiers quitting themselves like men (4:35).

1 Mac 4:36. The fight of 164 being successful, attention
could be given to the cult. Everyone knew that the shrine
at Mizpah would not do as a permanent home of the
liturgy, and there was a strong pressure group in the

community demanding the renewal of sacrifices in Jerusalem. The cult had to be returned to its proper setting
in the old temple. Judas and the army survey the temple
hill.

It is odd that the site should be a total wilderness, for
the old Syrian worship must have been performed in
some neat area, but anyway the Syrian slab had to be
tidied away and the courtyard swept, so the claim to have
renovated the place may not be wholly false.

The folk then celebrated the feast of the dedication,
Hanukkah, with lampstand, thurible and cup, the sacred
loaves were placed on the sacred table and the curtain
hung up before the empty holy place. Everyone was
happy. Everyone, that is, except the Syrians.

*1. Do we still see in lotteries, chance and divinations
among tea-leaves any connection with the Lord?*

*2. What would be our reaction if the present Israeli
authorities decided upon the renewal of animal sacrifices
in Jerusalem?*

1 Mac 5:1–7:18. Battle and intrigue

1 Mac 5:5. The old holy war ban is resurrected against
the men of a nomadic tribe who set upon Jewish travel-
lers to Jerusalem, but there is something not quite true
to the old usage in this invocation of the holiness of
Yahweh to protect the traders' merchandise.

1 Mac 5:43. Carnaim was not one of the more important
pagan shrines, and there is some dispute about its site.
Probably the town is the predecessor of Sheikh Sa'ad,
23 miles east of the Sea of Galilee. That the warriors
should race for such an unimportant shrine shows to what
plight they had come.

1 Mac 5:54. The army goes in procession up Mount Zion and offers a sacrifice to Yahweh there because no man has been killed. This wondrous safety is evidently the work of Yahweh, and the narrative has for some paragraphs after this a peculiarly religious vocabulary and tone. Israel's military force is gradually becoming aware of itself as Yahweh's army under the command of Yahweh's general. This new appreciation of Yahweh and his purposes is demonstrated negatively and positively:

(a) the non-Maccabean generals, Joseph and Azariah, are routed, and two thousand Israelites killed, because they went out against Judas' orders;

(b) the altars of the Philistine at Azotus are overturned as as a sign of the holiness of the Israelite campaign.

But the writer does not wholly abandon his naturalistic modes of explanation:

(a) the men defeated by Gorgias at Jamnia 'were not of the same stamp' as those who fought under Judas' command;

(b) the priests who, like Bishop Odo of Bayeux at Hastings, joined with Judas' warriors, were killed in the fight against the Philistine despite their sacred character, precisely because they were not properly trained for battle.

1 Mac 6:11. There is, of course, no proving, nor any wish to prove, the fictitious character of Antiochus' last speech to his assembled ministers, the friends of the King. But there cannot be a great deal of conviction about any assertion that Antiochus Epiphanes came to realise that his huge expedition against Persia had collapsed because he had so many years before set up an altar in the temple of his Jewish province and carried away the vessels of the Jewish priests.

It may be, and Polybius (31, 11) has a hint of this, that such thoughts went through the wandering mind of the king as he lay in his army tent, far from his soft palace bed, at the end of his 163 campaign across the Euphrates. Certainly the writer supposed that such thoughts ought to have come to the melancholy king at a moment of truth.

Antiochus knew that Demetrius, the son of Seleucus, might one day be released in Rome and come to claim his father's throne; he therefore made an effort to secure his own boy's inheritance by appointing Philip as the young king's governor. This attempt at forestalling of court rivalries did not come to anything. The dispute of Philip and Lysias concerning the protectorship so weakened the country that the Jews gained a respite from their besiegers, and Demetrius found the usurper's government unready to resist his coming.

1 Mac 6:18. After a note on the succession in Syria the writer continues his account of events at Jerusalem. The Akra had been a hampering factor in the Jews' discussion of how to establish their new state. In the summer of 163 Judas decided to clear the fortress of the Syrians and their quisling sympathisers, but his plans did not take enough account of the hellenisers among his own people. The garrison had friends in the city and these got word to Syria of what was going on in Jerusalem.

Antiochus v, or his governor Lysias, was convinced that the prestige of Syria was involved in this affair, and he sent troops to rescue his friends, and with the troops he sent the fearsome elephant. Judas' army ran away and the Syrians came to the walls of Mount Zion.

1 Mac 6:61. The grand array of fighting machines round the city is, in a most timely fashion, removed from the investiture of the walls, though pagan treachery spoils the climatic scene of reconciliation and religious freedom.

The writer, quite unlike the Deuteronomist or the Chronicler, does not think this a moment for elaborating a doctrinal proposition or a moral saw. He simply moves on to talk of the civil commotions of Philip, Antiochus, and Demetrius, for out of these alarums came the godless Alcimus, wearing the pectoral of the high priest.

1 Mac 7:16. At the oath-breaking the writer pauses to suggest that a scripture is being fulfilled (Ps 79 : 2–3). He is here employing past scripture as a source for comment on the present in an important manner. He is moving and he knows he is moving an old general statement into position for a particular effect. This is an early example of what became a common Jewish way with the scriptures. The past statement was said to be fulfilled not in the sense that the past speaker had had the present situation in mind long before it happened, but in the sense that the present was seen now to be in accord with the general wise view of things advanced by someone in the past. The present brought the past remark back into mind. The new testament is full of such things. Jesus' actions are repeatedly said to fulfil the scriptures. The evangelists do not mean that the old writers had Jesus in mind but that Jesus shows in actions the truth of that understanding of how things are exhibited in the old men's writings. The scriptures are not to be read that we may have confidence in Jesus, but Jesus' actions lead us to have confidence in the scriptures as accounts of the human situation.

1. The ban has disappeared from the wars of our society as a monstrous piece of savagery. Do we feel

*equally uncomfortable about the allies' demand in 1944
and 1945 of the enemies' 'unconditional surrender'?*

*2. Is it mere superstition to see in a piece of ill-fortune
a punishment for a previous offence against God?*

*3. Why do we read the old testament scriptures? Is it
simply to find a sign of Christ?*

1 Mac 7:19–9:22. Successes and final defeat of Judas

1 Mac 7:21. The writer sets down the miserable condition of the folk: murdered by Alcimus if they did not
support his claim to be the priest, and bullied by Judas if
they wandered away from his camps. It was no fun living
in Palestine that year.

1 Mac 7:35. While Alcimus and his Syrian friend, the
general Nicanor, reserved their threats and beatings for
the farmers they could manage the land well enough, but
when Alcimus came to the temple and mocked the sacred
liturgy of the clerics then he was in trouble. Prayers for
his violent downfall were offered at the sanctuary and
suddenly the business became not a political squabble but
a holy war.

1 Mac 7:41. Reminding Yahweh of the events of 2 Kg
18:17–19:37, Judas prayed for an angel to slaughter the
Syrians, and the fight at Adasa in 161 became a celebration of the divinely-gathered congregation. The trumpet
sounded and the men of Israel came out from their
villages to share in Yahweh's destruction of the pagan.

Nicanor's head is cut off as if he were another Sisera or
Holofernes. His hand, like that of Archbishop Cranmer,
becomes a symbol of his whole attitude of mind. A festival
is instituted which was kept on the anniversary of the

battle right up to Josephus' day (*Antiquities*, 12, 10, 5). Alcimus retired to Syria.

1 Mac 8:1. Judas sees that Jerusalem can profit from the Romans' dislike of Greek influence in the Near East, and the Romans see that Judas can do their work for them by keeping the Syrian power occupied with weakening engagements. The new importance of Judas' state can be gauged by his being thought a worthy ally by the Roman senate, and the new mode of carrying out the leadership of the Jewish community can be gauged by Judas' government wanting such an alliance because of 'the reputation of the Romans'. In earlier times the prophets had made great play with the foolishness of kings who relied upon Egypt or Nineveh for help in times of distress. Now no one seems to have thought the concept of alliance with the pagan foreigner out of place in a Jewish concept of the role of Jerusalem in the world.

The Jews, however, misjudged the meaning of the Roman treaty. The senate let them down when it came to the fight. And the Jews had heard a number of things about the senate which were quite false. The Jewish intelligence service evidently relied as much as any modern agency upon rumours of great power doings. The author of Maccabees sets down the Jewish beliefs without actually committing himself to the accuracy of the information they were using. Some elements of his account exemplify how rumours get from government sources to newspapers and then to history books and so become facts:

  (i) 8:4, Spain was declared part of the Roman territory in 201 but was certainly not mastered by the Romans at that time;

 (ii) 8:7, Antiochus the Great, defeated at Magnesia in 190, was not taken alive;

(iii) 8:8, 'India' and 'Media' are not to be taken seriously;
(iv) 8:15, the senate did not meet daily;
 (v) 8:16, there were two consuls.

1 Mac 8:23. The terms of this interesting treaty are obviously balanced in Rome's favour. The rhetoric of diplomacy does not conceal the fact that the Jews were required to assist in Rome's wars 'without recompense', and the Romans are to decide what help the Jews should have in their emergencies, and in most cases such help would be limited to keeping back supplies from Judas' enemies.

1 Mac 9:14. Judas is getting old and falls into an ancient trap set by Bacchides who must have been almost as surprised as he was delighted to see the ruse work to Judas' total ruin.

1 Mac 9:21. The little dirge of the people is reminiscent of the song for the dead Saul preserved in the *Book of the Just* (2 Sam 1:27).

1. Do we now feel uncomfortable in the face of symbolic gestures like Cranmer's thrusting his hand into the fire 'for it first offended'?

2. What symbolic gestures are to be found in our own society, and do they any longer bear significance?

3. Does it affect our view of the writer of 1 Maccabees if we 'catch him out' in an historical error?

3

Jonathan
1 Mac 9:23–12:53

1 Mac 9:23. Now everything goes wrong. The old hellenisers come out of their libraries and country manor houses and start talking of modern discoveries by Greek scientists, modern paintings by Greek artists, and modern fashions by Greek dress designers. The country goes to the games, the horses, and the dogs.

After the failure of the crops it must have seemed as if the very soil was in league with these new men, for they were able to blame the old regime for the economic mess while they continued themselves to eat well on the subsidies they accepted from the Syrian government. The hellenisers enjoyed both bread and games.

The poor men of the old order, Jonathan and Simon, the Hasmonaeans, and their supporters, were forced to camp out in the desert; and when Jonathan sent his brother John to escort their women and children and family possessions to the friendly Nabataeans, they looked such a defenceless crew as they passed the stronghold of Madaba, that brigands swooped down on them and captured the lot.

The vengeance the Hasmonaeans exacted was achieved not by a national punitive expedition but by a piece of family cunning. Life was getting wilder in the desert. And as the avengers, decked in the gaudy wraps of the

Jambrian wedding party, went singing back to their
camp, they were surprised by the Syrian army at the
Jordan ford. The Jews had to make a fight of it before
they were able to reach the bank and swim across to their
camp. A great deal of the booty from the raid on the wedding guests must have been left on the nearer bank. A
man is unlikely to hold such kickshaws above his head
as he swims for his life amid a hail of spears.

However many men Bacchides lost at the river fight he
had enough to garrison forts up and down the country.

1 Mac 9:54. Alcimus evidently wanted to bring down
the wall of separation between Jew and Gentile in order
that they might worship together, if not in spirit and in
truth then at least in the syncretism of a hellenised
temple. His death in 159 brought all such efforts to an
end.

Bacchides, having made sure of the military command
of the country, had no great interest in the religious
squabbles that Alcimus had led him into. When Alcimus
died and the city was securely garrisoned Bacchides
decided that there was nothing left for him to do in
Jerusalem and in 157 he made a peace with the orthodox
and went home to the Syrian court for a well-earned
leave. That he did not care to come out of this pleasant
staff-officer retirement at headquarters appears in the
sequel when he became furious with the hellenisers for
making it necessary for him to march his men about
Palestine again.

1 Mac 10:1–11:62

The rival claimants to the Seleucid throne began in 152
to bid for Jewish support.

(a) Demetrius, recognising the political independence of Jerusalem, withdrew his troops from Judaea and allowed Jonathan to occupy the city;

(b) Alexander Balas, who claimed to be a son of Antiochus Epiphanes, could offer no less than Demetrius, so political independence is assured by both sides, and to top Demetrius' kindness, Alexander sent Jonathan the insignia of the high priest, appointing him to be one of the king's friends;

(c) Demetrius attempted to outbid Alexander by adding to the offer of prestige those of economic advantage, remitting the substantial tribute that the Jews had been paying the central Syrian government, and sending home the Jews held prisoner in his territories.

In the end Jonathan backed Alexander and became one of his chief supporters. The Jewish leader was received with honour by both Alexander and his father-in-law Ptolemy of Egypt.

The younger Demetrius' campaign to grab the Seleucid throne is said in chapter 10 to have been defeated by Jonathan, and certainly the Jew seems to have been a better ally to Alexander than his Egyptian father-in-law. That wily gentleman not only put his own troops to occupy Alexander's fortresses but, having daughternapped Alexander's wife, he gave her to his new ally, Demetrius. Alexander was defeated and fled to his friends in Arabia, who promptly cut off his head and sent it to Ptolemy. The joy of Egypt was so unbounded that he died, perhaps of a heart-attack on receiving the head, three days later. What his daughter felt is not recorded.

Nor, more strangely, are we told what Jonathan thought of all this dropping-down-dead. Despite the mutterings of the hellenisers the Hasmonaean prince was confirmed as high priest by the new king, Demetrius II.

Demetrius II wrote to his backer, the Cretan Lasthenes, whom he termed with customary oriental flattery 'his father', reporting the lands and monies arrangements with Jonathan. This referring back to his Cretan sponsor is an indication of the powerful foreign influence in the new king's court. And resentment against this influence among the Syrian military officers was increased by the king's refusal to dismiss the Cretan mercenaries on his staff.

An attempt of the Antiocheans to revolt against Demetrius II and his friends was thwarted by the Jewish troops Jonathan had sent to protect the king, but Demetrius proved ungrateful and did not pay Jonathan for the brigade. It may be that he thought the Jewish guards had collected quite enough for themselves when they sacked Antioch after putting down the citizens' revolt. Demetrius was a fool. Jonathan was persuaded by the king's meanness to go over to the camp of his rival, Antiochus VI, Dionysius, the young son of Alexander. This boy had been looked after by an Arab friend of his father and the Syrian general Trypho. In his changing of loyalties Jonathan was joined by the Syrian veterans in Antioch, and together they ousted Demetrius II from his capital.

1 Mac 11:63. So prominent had Jonathan and his brother Simon become among Antiochus VI's supporters that the generals of Demetrius invaded Galilee and were with some difficulty pushed out of the country.

1 Mac 11:70. The description of the fight at Hazor is a splendid example of the writer's desire to make these army matters a little more religious. In this account the

holy war situation of a small number of troops (only three
of them in this affair) penance and prayer, leads into a
total rout of the enemy. It cannot have been quite like
this.

1 Mac 12:5. The general tone of the letter sent to the
Spartans is designed to encourage a belief that religious
orthodoxy is linked with military victory. The Spartans
are told that men with 'the holy books' and 'the support
of heaven' do not need allies, but that they like being
friends with everyone, and pray for the Spartans 'on
every occasion' at the Jewish festivals.

An interest of the letter now is its demonstration of a
belief in a universal brotherhood of men and a prayer for
that brotherhood in the temple. The Spartans had
already made a pleasant bow to universalist niceties and
accepted a rhetorical kinship with the children of
Abraham.

The letters to the senate and the council of Sparta
were sent by the authority of Jonathan the high priest
and the *Gerousia,* the council of elders in Jerusalem
(cf the old institution of Deut 17:8–13, and the more
recent council set up by Jehoshaphat, 2 Chron 19:8).
This body was developed later into the sanhedrin, having final power on a great many matters of civil and
religious interest in Jerusalem, but at this time it is
evident that Jonathan could deploy the members of the
council as he wished and that there was no real authority
other than that exercised and delegated by the high priest
and army chief of staff.

1 Mac 12:24. Jonathan was spreading his power in other
ways besides the ordering of general prayer and diplomatic missions. He led an army to Hamath on the middle
reaches of the Orontes against the generals of Demetrius,

and another to the north of Damascus against the Zaba-
deans. And such aggrandisement lent colour to Trypho's
fear that Jonathan would have to be reckoned with if a
change of kings were plotted.

Jonathan was certainly losing his grip. First Demetrius'
blustering generals frighten him with false fire as if he
were a mere pagan with no divine aid at all, and then
Antiochus' shifty general tricks him into the spider's
parlour. It seems to be characteristic of the Hasmonaean
heroes that they suddenly fall for an old trick and walk
into an unsubtle death. Judas was caught by the old
military device of a mock retreat, and now Jonathan is
bamboozled into surrendering himself to his enemy.

Trypho carts Jonathan around with him and plays
ransom games with his younger brother Simon until in
a fit of temper at an inconvenient fall of snow he kills his
prisoner and goes grumbling back to his own country.
The tomb of the Maccabees was standing in the writer's
time, and fragments of it have survived to our own day,
but that can be little comfort to the Hasmonaeans.

*1. Why do stories of blood and thunder and brigands
retain their interest for such quiet peaceful persons as
ourselves?*

*2. What content do we give such a phrase as 'universal
brotherhood'?*

*3. What significance is there for us in the erection of
a tomb-stone or memorial? Do we want one for ourselves?*

4

Simon
1 Mac 13:1–16:24

1 Mac 13:31. Antiochus VI was killed by Trypho when he got home in an angry mood, and Simon, realising that he was unlikely to gain much from conversations with the usurper, turned his allegiance to Demetrius II. In 142 Demetrius recognised Simon as the high priest of Jerusalem and one of the king's friends. He composed their alliance by abandoning every claim to tax the Jews.

The general feeling in Jerusalem at this time was that Simon had brought to a happy close the years of struggle. There seemed to be a chance that the victories of Judas and Jonathan would be followed by a new age of peace and prosperity. The declaration of a new calendar era is an expression of this high optimism.

1 Mac 13:43. The writer too delights in the new thing. Simon is immediately shown to have a care of all things cultic. The capture of Gezer is the occasion of a ritual purification of the city, the burning of the hellenistic idols, the chanting of psalms in praise of Yahweh and the allocation of land and houses to men who were known to be servants of the law.

1 Mac 13:49. Similarly the occupation of the Akra, the last and strongest citadel of the pagans in Palestine, is celebrated after the ritual purification by a religious procession of musicians and singers, much like the dancing entrance of the ark arranged by David.

1 Mac 14:5. The poem in praise of Simon is a gathering of older biblical phrases and, though probably put together quite hurriedly as an obituary psalm for Simon's funeral procession, is used by the writer to suggest that the land is still waiting for that prophet who would know what to do with all the disparate elements of life in contemporary Jerusalem (cf 1 Mac 4:46). The historical references at the beginning of the song to Simon's exploits at Joppa, Gezer and other cities lead into an idyllic account of what might one day be realised in Israel—a time when the old men might dream dreams, the young men enjoy the elegance of youth, and the nation gather the harvest at peace before making together the pilgrimage to Yahweh's temple in Jerusalem.

1 Mac 14:16. The references to Rome and Sparta have almost a doublet quality, reminding the reader of Judas' diplomatic efforts, but the detail of the shield-bearing Numenius in verse 24 (which should be read in its original place before verse 16) suggests that Simon did confirm the old alliance by a special embassy.

1 Mac 14:25. The establishment of Simon as high priest for ever is celebrated in hellenistic style with the assumption of the purple, the erection of a memorial tablet in the temple itself, and the minting of coins bearing the ethnarch's head.

On the capture of his brother, Demetrius II, by the Persians in 139, Antiochus VII, Sidetes, decided to assume the royal dignities and rule in Antioch. He recognised Simon's independence, accepting the political facts and making a show of granting Simon the power of coining money which the Hasmonaean had already taken for himself. Antiochus VII left Simon unmolested in Jerusalem while he chased Trypho out of Syrian territory, but when he felt himself to be in control of the areas once in rebel hands, Antiochus turned on Simon and his Jews and demanded the return of territories Simon had appropriated during the reign of Demetrius II, and the return of Syrian troops to the akra. Simon, secure in his magnificence, would not give up anything to the Syrian ambassador and prepared for war. The command of the Jewish military force was given to Simon's son, John.

John proved himself an able successor of his father and uncles, both in his defeat of the Syrian army on that expedition, and his quick grip of power in Palestine in the treacherous situation which followed upon the murder of his father and brothers at Dok.

The writer concluded his account of the Hasmonaean family with yet another of the great men being killed by a trickster, and yet another hero rising to leadership in Jerusalem and continuing the Jewish effort towards national independence under the law. But cultural influences are not so easily defeated as foreign armies. The Jews had begun by objecting to the hellenists' attacks on the orthodox life style, the crusade ended with Simon observing the law certainly, but recognised as a member of the Roman imperial society and living a life of tremendous luxury in the style of contemporary hellenistic princes all over the east.

Worse was to come in the later reigns of the Hasmonaean kings.

1. Must those who go to war against a culture inevitably come to accept the life style of their enemy?

2. Does there seem to be a general purpose shaping the composition of 1 Maccabees?

2 Maccabees

Introduction

This book covers again the events described in 1 Maccabees 1–7 and, apart from the letters at the beginning, was
probably written in Greek, possibly by an Alexandrian
Jew, and perhaps in the first century BC.

The writer of 1 Maccabees seems to have been a Sad-
ducee, our present epitomist is probably an early
Pharisee, a man of the Hasidic tradition who cared more
than the writer of 1 Maccabees for such legal matters as
the regulations against fighting on the sabbath (cf 1 Mac
2:41, 9:43 and 2 Mac 6:11, 8:25, 12:38, 15:1) and the
doctrine of the resurrection of the dead (cf the silence at
1 Mac 2:51, 3:59, 9:9, and the affirmation of 2 Mac
7:9, 7:14, 7:23, 7:36 and 12:43).

Our epitomist makes rather more than the writer of
1 Maccabees of the temple worship, and particularly of
the celebration of the feast of *Hanukkah*. At his description of the origins of this commemoration of the purification of the temple he departs from the version of events
presented at 1 Maccabees (cf 1 Mac 1:54–9, 4:52 with
2 Mac 1:11–18, 9:1–10:9), a departure not wholly to be
accounted for by the fact that 2 Maccabees is set out
according to a chronology which reckons each event as
happening one year before their rating in 1 Maccabees.

Besides *Hanukkah* the epitomist is interested in the

feasts of *Nicanor* (named after the Syrian general, 15.27–35) and *Purim* (celebrating the justification of Mordecai —2 Mac 15:36, cf Esther). These are all cultic realisations of that divine protection of Jewry exhibited also in the granting of heavenly apparitions (2:21 and 15:11), the sending of angels to fight for the Jews' cause (11:6, 15:23), the golden horsemen of Yahweh (3:25, 10:29, 11:8), and finally demonstrated in the equity of reward and punishment for individuals (4:38, 5:10, 6:12, 13:4–8 etc), and for the nation (5:17–40, 12:40), both here and hereafter (7:9 ff, 12:43). The providence and justice of Yahweh are brought into mind by the liturgical celebration of history; as we join in the prayer and song of the people we are brought to realise that Yahweh will make all things well 'in the end'.

There is, therefore, in the epitomist's view a direct connection between now and for ever, and the bridge between the present and the eternal is manifest in the liturgy. Life after death is the final movement of the process begun in history and continued in social morality and cultic festivity. Survival of the individual beyond the grave seems to the epitomist the only proper vindication of divine justice and human action.

The epitomist delights in religious doctrines. His work is replete with modern instances of everlasting truths. He means his account of Judas to bring home to his reader the glorious truth that in the liturgy he may meet Yahweh the Lord of history, and come himself to share in the divine process as it continues in the present.

1

Letters and preface
2 Mac 1:1–2:32

2 Mac 1:1–2:18. Letters

2 Mac 1:1. The first prefatory letter was sent as a greeting to the Egyptian Jews, urging them not to loose their hold on the common covenant tradition, and proclaiming the law as effective outside the frontiers of the holy land. This letter ends at verse 7b with the name of the reigning king and the date of dispatch, 169. The events it describes are those set down in 1 Mac 1:39, 4:38 and 2 Mac 8:33, but it is noteworthy that the writers do not allude to the battles fought under Judas' leadership. The people's prayer for Yahweh's aid is the deciding factor in the situation.

2 Mac 1:7b. The second prefatory letter is an appeal to the Jews in Egypt to celebrate the feast of the dedication of the temple after its purification by Judas. Two textual points are of interest here:

(a) the feast of tabernacles referred to here is not the famous autumn feast in the month of Tishri, but the feast in the month of Chislev which had some cultic features much like those of the true tabernacles;

(b) the letter should be assigned to the period immediately after Judas' victory in 148, not 188, and it is certainly older than the letter placed first in the manuscript.

2 Mac 1:10. The third prefatory letter is another invitation to the feast of the dedication (cf verse 18). Since it is addressed to Aristobulus, a philosopher who allegorised the Pentateuch for Ptolemy Philometer, it must have been sent before the news arrived of the great man's death in 144 BC.

2 Mac 1:14. The letter ought by any ordinary chronology to be describing the death of Antiochus Epiphanes, but the details are taken from the account of the death of Antiochus the Great. Perhaps the writer thought that Antiochus Epiphanes being at least as wicked as Antiochus the Great should properly suffer at least as horribly at his end.

2 Mac 1:18. The miracle of the fire is nowhere else recorded in the old testament but is not the less likely for that. Evidently something of a naphtharic nature was brought from Persia for the kindling of the sacrificial materials preserved from the old temple. Those who had gone into exile would have learnt something of their captors' fire-worship and its practices, and certainly it is not unlikely that a Persian ruler would have accepted the sacredness of a place where such things happened.

Naphtar has connotations with a verb 'to separate', and the writer of the letter, exercising that talent for inventive etymology characteristic of the Hebrews, sees in the coming of the strange stuff a heavenly separation of the secular and the sacred.

2 Mac 2:1. The story of Jeremiah and the ark is perhaps suggested by some remarks in the epistle of Jeremiah 'against the idols' in Baruch, a deuterocanonical work not in the Hebrew bible (cf Baruch 6). There must have been all sorts of cultic legends of how the ark came to be lost or hidden. It was not conceivable that so great a sign of Yahweh's presence could have been destroyed out of the world for ever.

The purpose of telling the story here is evidently to give a sanction to a temple without an ark, and to encourage men to come to the festival of dedication with some confidence that this is indeed the shrine whose history goes back to Solomon's temple and Moses' fire. The whole of 2 Maccabbees is written as a justification of the cult in this holy place.

1. There has been for some decades a fashion for the integration of the sacred and the secular. What have been the results of this attempt?

2. Is there some inherent necessity for a liturgy's effectiveness in the community that it be able to establish its connection with the past ritual? Do men come easily to accept the idea of a liturgy being new?

2 Mac 2:19–32. Preface

2 Mac 2:19. The epitomist now rehearses the story which gives the justification for the feast. The history of Judas coresponds here to those happy legends by which pagan shrines all over the Near East gave warrant to their cults. Similar impulses can be discovered in the foundation stories of later shrines. That of Westminster Abbey is typical of mediaeval examples. The Lourdes story is a more modern instance. They all have the form: that which happened here renders the place holy and ensures the continuance of divine protection at this place, let us then erect a shrine here for ourselves and our descendants.

The epitomist thinks of Judas primarily as one who purified the site, set up the altar and celebrated the feast, and only secondarily as the man who fought fights enough to make the liturgy possible.

2 Mac 2:24. A whole dustbin of theories of 'how inspiration works' has failed to take account of this description of the epitomist's self-awareness. His work has been a great fag for him. He has been a drudge for others, and anyone who suggests that divine aid relieved him of most of the work may be sure that if such an opinion had been uttered in the epitomist's hearing the critic would have come away with a sore head.

   1. Do we still require a sacred place in which to worship? What do we intend by our talk of a worship 'in spirit and in truth'?
   2. What do we mean when we say that the scriptures are 'inspired'? (cf Hamish Swanston, Community Witness, *London 1967, ch 1).*

2
Stories, edifying and tall
2 Mac 3:1–15:39

2 Mac 3:1. The history of Heliodorus is marvellously well told, and it would be a philistine act to question too closely the factual worth of the story of the old priest in his vestments, ashen and palsied at the thought of the sacrilege, the young girls fluttering like frightened birds at the windows, the swaggering pagan general, and the sudden overturning of every human category at the vision of the golden horsemen and the bright twins with their whips.

Certain it is that the Syrian kings needed money after the Roman exactions in 188 DC, and certain that the hellenist and conservative factions among the leading men of the Jews would be likely enough to betray each other to the foreigner, and certain also that Heliodorus was a proud man quite capable of carrying out the business in so boorish a manner, for he was bold enough to murder his master Seleucus IV, and seek to make himself king during the minority of Seleucus' son, Demetrius. Set a thief to catch a thief. Poachers make the best game-keepers. Heliodorus was ousted by another such as himself, Antiochus IV Epiphanes. For the rest we ought simply to sit back and enjoy a brilliantly-told tale of Yahweh and his way with the wicked.

2 Mac 4:1. The rivalries of Simon and Onias led to the high priest travelling to Antioch in hopes that an appeal to Antiochus would settle everything in Jerusalem. But while he was gone Onias' brother Jason seized the office and the treasury, consolidating his position by promising the king further funds, and declaring his total commitment to the hellenisation of Jerusalem. He erected a gymnasium where the young men ran naked, and encouraged his younger priests to join an athletic club dedicated to Hermes. The epitomist has a keen sense of moral retribution and delights in the disaster Jason piled up for himself and his young hellenist clerics.

2 Mac 4:18. The high priest even sent money to pay for sacrifices at the altar of Hercules. This god was that same Tyrian Melkart that Jezebel had worshipped and whose priests Elijah had had lynched at Carmel. Jason was defying Yahweh in the name of a god who had been trounced long ago. Some terrible punishment would obviously come quickly.

The craft of Menelaus was great enough to bring death to Onias, the avaricious vizier Andronicus, the temple robber Lysimachus, and a number of the leaders of the outraged orthodox in Jerusalem, and even at last to the old plotter Jason in his Arabian exile, for Menelaus understood the giving of bribes, and the gentle art of survival.

Menelaus' greatest cleverness was his management of affairs so that it always appeared that he was defending the royal authority of Antiochus Epiphanes. The king decided to deal with those who had troubled the peace of his province, and encouraged by Menelaus he sacked Jerusalem and the temple itself. The epitomist accounts for Yahweh's allowing this terrible event by noting the sinfulness of the population which had forsaken the law.

1. *What is it about twins that makes them so often in African and Graeco-Roman mythologies the bearers of divine messages and the effectors of divine intent?*

2. *What explanations might be offered to account for the fact that it was the priesthood which led the people in the adoption of hellenistic manners?*

2 Mac 6:1. Antiochus put some energy now into the prosecution of a hellenisation of Jerusalem and the Jews. He appointed governors to see that the cultural life of the province was brought into line with that of the rest of his territories, and the population of the city was rendered helpless by the sabbath day massacre.

2 Mac 6:12. The epitomist's theory of history and other nations' enjoyment of undeserved prosperity is based on an eschatological concept of punishment. It is better to be punished for sin as history goes on than to have to account for all transgressions at the end. Yahweh's favour includes his granting the Jews a long history in which to pay off their debts.

2 Mac 6:18. The description of the martyrdom of Eleazar makes a moving story even for those who cannot appreciate the erection of dietary rules to the high status of principle. It is to be noticed that Eleazar certainly believes in the survival of a man beyond the grave, survival at least for punishment if not reward.

2 Mac 7:9. The same belief, together with an expectation of being 'raised up' is witnessed in the cry of the second son, and in the seventh son's picture of the heavenly banquet.

The story of the seven sons, which somehow became attached to the Maccabean family chronicle though it had no original connection with the descendants of Mattathias, is a beautifully managed piece of literature. There is room enough, of course, for all kinds of doubts about its factual character. Everything comes so trippingly, every feature is so pat for the purposes of the narrative, every character so properly bad or good in the extreme, that it would be unreasonable not to admit an amount of editing at the least. That is to say, the epitomist has taken some pains to make his work pleasant for the reader.

The story is nicely structured, each brother adding to the argument which must sustain all Jews under persecution, and Yahweh's justice being fully vindicated by the sixth son's acknowledging his own sin and his faith that the tyrant will suffer for his treatment of the servants of the law.

The mother's speech is interesting as the first reference in the surviving Jewish literature of an established belief in creation 'out of nothing'. This is a refinement upon the doctrine of creation contained in the Genesis narrative of how God managed the waters of chaos.

2 Mac 7:45. The story now has reached the moment when the redeemer must appear and justify the family's faith in Yahweh's love and power. There has been enough of torture.

2 Mac 8:1. And on cue, in a carefully patterned piece of narrative, we are told of the hidden coming of Judas Maccabees and his companions. The revolt begins and prospers. One after another victories come fast. 'The temple' is now the rallying cry of a triumphant army which begins its campaign by listening to the reading of the law.

2 Mac 8:25. Every human category is overturned. Those who planned to purchase slaves are themselves captured and their money taken as the victors' booty; those professional soldiers who dressed in their fine armour are stripped by their rough adversaries, those who had felt themselves deserted are reconciled to Yahweh, and the man who wore the purple robes of state runs naked like an escaping slave to his hide-out.

The striking balance obtained by placing such victories immediately after the stories of degrading torture is certainly to be credited to the epitomist. He knew what to include and what to omit from his original source material.

The epitomist enjoys such an heroic conversion of events and sets in apposition happy phrases of defeat and victory for his description of the last hours of the hated Antiochus Epiphanes. He was indebted perhaps for one element in his account of Antiochus to his reading of Aeschylus' *Persae* and its famous image of the tyrant who would thrash the waves, and a Hebrew would join this classical image of pride with a remembrance of Yahweh's exodus command of the waters.

The image of the divine lash may have been cherished by the epitomist from the accounts he had of the episode of Heliodorus who had prophesied that anyone who attempted to attack the city of the temple would be flogged by divine powers (2 Mac 3:38).

1. Do we approve without any reservation at all the way in which martyrdom is celebrated by the epitomist? Would we want our daughter to marry a martyrable man?

2. The mother expresses her belief in creation out of nothing. What meaning does this bear for us?

2 Mac 9:19. It would seem likely that Antiochus wrote similar letters to all his provincial governors. In other copies we should, if they were extant, read 'Syrians' or 'Phoenicians' for 'Jews' in our copy.

Antiochus needed, like the father of Maria Theresa, some promise from the great men of his empire to ensure the succession of his son. There were claimants enough to provide excuses for civil wars, and Antiochus must have had a disquietening idea of the ambitions of men like Philip and Lysias.

2 Mac 10:1. At the death of the old tyrant the Jews could take advantage of the crisis in Syrian affairs to look after their own interests. They could now go to the temple without looking over their shoulder for the Syrian horsemen. The feast of dedication is celebrated and all is well. The epitomist has arrived at the climax of his story. He has given an account of the events which led to that feast to which the writers of those letters set at the beginning of the book had invited the Jews of Egypt.

2 Mac 10:25. The army of Timotheus is frightening enough for a day of penance and supplication to be ordered, and the Jews are answered by the vision of the five horsemen who routed the pagan, and after some exertion themselves the Jews can close the campaign with a hymn and a prayer.

2 Mac 11:5. A similar sequence of penance and prayer in Jerusalem, a heavenly rider, and a battle of some fierceness leads to the defeat of Lysias, and the proclamation of peace in the land.

These episodes bring the events close to conformity with the holy war pattern. After the stories of the nasty plots of Joppa and Jamnia, the epitomist recounts an attack on Caspin at which the Jews showed themselves to be aware of their inheritance of the old covenant life.

2 Mac 12:15. They invoke Yahweh the destroyer of Jericho, the Lord of the armies of Israel, and trust him to overthrow the gentile. And their prayer is answered.

2 Mac 12:37. After this, and the hymn-singing at the battle against Gorgias, and the general purification, and the observance of the sabbath, the epitomist relates the story of the dead men of Adullam who lay unburied on the field because their comrades knew that they had been slaughtered for their sin in wearing the pagan amulets. The holy war ethos is established as the setting for the new doctrine of prayer for the dead who are to live again.

It does not seem necessary to enter into the political ups and downs of Jew and Syrian, the punishment at last of Menelaus, or the much-debated matter of whether Razis' death justifies a modern suicide. These are all matters that are clear enough to those intelligent readers whom the epitomist hoped to instruct and delight.

1. Queen Victoria became impatient when at a time of national crisis the Archbishop of Canterbury suggested a day of penance. Do we share her belief that a day of work would be more effective?

2. What do we believe we effect by our prayers for the dead?